Nancy —

Thank again
being my proof-reader!

Thanks for being a
wonderful support to me in
my endeavors. You are a
true friend!

Love!
"Maggie"
(AKA Bon)

The Dementia Diary

The Dementia Diary

Maggie Anderson

To order additional copies of this book, contact:
Xlibris
1-888-795-4274
www.Xlibris.com
Orders@Xlibris.com
739913

January, week 1

I got a call today from Mom's clinic requesting that I accompany her to an appointment next week. Even though they assured me there was nothing serious going on, there's an ominous feeling that hangs over their request. Mom's health has been unbelievably good, even at the age of eight-five now. She only began taking a medication for high blood pressure and a drug for osteoporosis prevention a couple of years ago. I think that's pretty amazing to make it into your eighties before needing any medication.

Mom had taken a fall just after Christmas and did quite a number on her face. She had two black eyes. She has always been on the vain side and a couple of years ago refused to undergo eyelid surgery, even after her droopy lid began to impair her vision and therefore would be covered under insurance. Her excuse was that she didn't want to have a black eye. Even with thick makeup, the bruising and swelling from this recent fall were obvious a week later. She couldn't remember how she fell (it happened during the night) but thought maybe she had tripped on her bedspread getting up to visit the bathroom. She also complained of rib pain when she called me the morning after the incident, so I took her to Urgent Care at that point. After several hours, the verdict was simply bruising, nothing broken. Maybe that's what they want to discuss, since it's the second fall in a year. I'll have to wait and see. I'll call my sister, Karen, and let her know what's going on.

Karen and I have enjoyed Mom's good health, spending many weekends taking little excursions and the occasional several-day trips to Las Vegas or the Cranberry Fest in Wisconsin. The three of us travel well together and have gotten a couple of trips in each year for the past twenty years. Usually, Karen and I talk nonstop and laugh often to the point of tears. We agreed we got our sense of humor from Dad; Mom doesn't often get the joke but joins in the laughter anyway. Sometimes Mom is the butt of the joke but usually doesn't seem to realize it. We aren't obvious or cruel in our teasing; it's subtle. Mom is a good sport; she is quick to laugh and eager to join in our antics. We always wanted to document our trips in photos but found it difficult to get the three of us in one picture, thus began our practice of taking pictures of our reflections in any large mirror or window we came across. We would be anxious to get the film developed so we could laugh at the pictures where our heads were all cut off or there were three little heads at the very bottom of the photo. We had so much fun and treasured the memories made on these trips.

Mom just recently retired! With nothing more than a high school education, she climbed the ladder at the bank where she began as a teller at age forty to secure a position as a loan officer. She was a professional, acting and looking the part. She's always been a very classy lady, so put together with her wardrobe and accessories. She is extremely attractive for someone her age and has had many suitors, though she is not interested one iota. She still drives and has lived alone for forty years. It's been like aging was for someone else, not my mother.

I can't help but wonder if we are approaching a new chapter in our relationship. I have enjoyed the status quo and don't want it to change. I wonder what issues may have arisen. I will try not to let my imagination get the better of me.

January, week 2

Mom seemed a bit irritated that I was summoned to accompany her to the appointment. She was annoyed and confused. She couldn't imagine what the reason would be. Mom was actually rather rude to the doctor, which is so out of character for her. She is normally beyond pleasant, sweet and charming to the point of being obnoxious. Mom avoided eye contact with him and was very curt with her answers—that is, when she felt moved to respond at all. It was shocking to witness. For the first time in my life, I felt I was in "role-reversal," urging her to behave.

Dr. Miller addressed the recent history of Mom's falling and commented on her memory issues. Maybe what irritated Mom was that we were talking about her, right in front of her, not talking with her. She literally growled, "My memory is just fine!" I had to admit to Dr. Miller that I hadn't noticed memory lapses. Mom has always liked attention and seems to think the little-old-lady routine is cute and funny. I thought she was being silly and annoying; I didn't think she was serious.

The doctor recommended we make an appointment with a neurologist to have some testing done. He gave the usual warning against worry, the ruling-things-out mantra. From the records, he was aware that Mom had two daughters, and he suggested either one or both of us should accompany Mom to help with the interview and share any concerns or observations. I haven't had any concerns other than being more impatient with her lately.

Taking Mom to another doctor should be a real challenge! Mom is not exactly agreeable with this plan. I'm thinking we should make a day of it—lunch, a little shopping, a visit to the neurologist—just a normal day of Mom with her two daughters.

January, week 3

The manager of Mom's senior apartment building called and wants to do an article on Mom for their newsletter. They are celebrating their thirtieth year, and Mom was one of the first residents. He had some facts from Mom and wanted clarification and a few more details. She had told him that Karen and I had enjoyed annual trips to the casino in Hinckley. Hinckley? That's a Minnesota Native American casino. We used to go to Las Vegas annually. I think I took Mom to Hinckley once on a day trip. I thought that was odd that she would confuse a plane ride to Vegas with a car ride to Hinckley.

She also had neglected to tell him that she was very active in the American Business Women Association when she was employed as a bank officer and served as president one year. In her curio, right in front, was a statue with a brass plaque stating "Woman of the Year." She had always been very proud of that accomplishment.

I guess Dr. Miller may have something. She may be experiencing some "memory issues."

I told the building manager a few more details on Mom for the article and corrected some of the information he got from her. He invited us to join the celebration in a couple of weeks. Normally, I wouldn't want to spend time with all the elderly residents, but I may want to observe Mom in her natural habitat. My husband, Allen, probably won't want to attend, but I think Karen will want to be there, especially after I fill her in on the conversation with the apartment manager.

January, week 4

It was Sunday, so Mom came over to our house for dinner and a game or two of Dominos Mexican Train (our routine going on eight years). I make dinner, while Mom tries to make small talk with Allen. She seems to make the same statement every week. She will walk in the door and say, "That sure was a big newspaper today." She may think she's telling him, "Job well done," since he's employed by the newspaper.

I noticed she had the same outfit on that she wore the day before and the Sunday before that. She's always been so stylish; this repeat of clothing puzzled me. Her hair and makeup are perfection, and her wardrobe is high-end fashion. More recently, though still fashionable, she has begun to wear the same couple of outfits repeatedly. I know she has dozens of outfits, so for her to limit herself to one seems unusual.

Out of the routine, the boys and their girlfriends joined us this Sunday, so there were seven of us playing dominos. This resulted in conversation during the game. Mom wanted us to stay on task and take our turns in a timely fashion. If conversation caused us to lapse a bit, she would loudly order, "Take your turn! Take your turn!" This fun game has apparently evolved into a very serious activity for her. Mom has become quite the stickler for the rules and will verbally attack at the slightest provocation. We've dubbed her "the Dominos Police."

The boys laugh it off, and Allen, who seems to have less patience with her than I do, just shakes his head.

February, week 1 (five weeks)

Karen and I both accompanied Mom to the neurologist. The doctor was a pleasant woman of Middle Eastern origin. Since Mom was not on board with this program, her attitude was less than cordial; top that off with not being able to readily understand the doctor because of her accent, it made for an embarrassing hour of Mom acting out. She heaved sighs, rolled her eyes, and muttered under her breath constantly. Our efforts to control her were futile, only causing her obvious annoyance. Karen and I shot desperate glances to each other, both sharing the other's frustration and feelings of helplessness.

Prior to this appointment, Karen and I discussed that we had both noticed some oddities in Mom's behavior over the last few months. A common experience was her irritability and impatience with waitstaff when we'd take her out to eat. Today, she was showing this same irritability, but we had never seen her this bad. We just didn't know how to react.

One of the tests they gave Mom was a "Mini-Mental," where they asked a series of questions and required Mom to perform some actions and problem solving. I wanted so badly to shout out the answers! I know who the president is! I know that drawing was of a rhinoceros, not a cow! I know where to place the hands on the clock to indicate ten after the hour! I could remember the three words given at the beginning! All three—not just two! Watching Mom struggle to figure things out was downright painful. I wanted to help but knew I shouldn't.

Another appointment had to be made for more intensive testing. We will again both be accompanying Mom to that appointment. A hearing test was also ordered, which Karen will take her to. The doctor assumes Mom doesn't hear the question; I think Mom is ignoring her out of disdain.

Karen and I talked on the phone later that evening. We were equally shocked at Mom's inability to process. Mom performed so poorly on the test. How had we not noticed this before?

February, week 2 (six weeks)

The testing today was "occupational." Mom was asked to perform tasks like making a piece of toast, filling a weekly pill box, and using the telephone to order flowers. She did not want to use the phone. Since it was a standardized test, refusing to complete any part of it would greatly affect the scoring. I was trying to explain to Mom why she had to perform this action, but Karen was upset by what she perceived as Mom's desperation and temporarily left the room. Later she shared with me that she suspects Mom has forgotten how to use the phone. She felt empathy for her in the testing, and she just couldn't stay and watch it.

The results of the testing will be sent to Dr. Miller, and we made a follow-up appointment with the neurologist. We also made an appointment for a simulated driving test, since they are concerned about her operating a motor vehicle at her age. Thoughtfully, they didn't want to do all the testing at one time.

These appointments and tests are hard on Mom. She doesn't like them and expresses that intensely. Trying to explain the point of it all to her is difficult, since she insists there is nothing wrong with her. She feels like we are all conspiring against her for some strange reason. I'm sympathetic to her, yet I get so frustrated trying to get her to understand what is going on.

February, week 3 (seven weeks)

Karen and I picked up Mom for the final (we hope) test that would involve the driving simulator. She was waiting in her apartment lobby for us. She had on the same outfit as the week before; she may have been wearing different earrings.

All the way to the clinic, she kept asking where we were going and why. Several times we took turns explaining the doctor's concern about her age and driving. She insisted she was a good driver and this testing thing was ridiculous. We agreed with her and advised she do her best to prove it to them.

The mock vehicle was a large wood box with a seat, steering wheel, pedals, and mirrors. It was a crude replica of a car. The first thing Mom did once seated in the device was to place both feet on the pedals. The instructor excitedly asked if this is how she drove all the time. The answer was no; this was a strange toy-looking apparatus that she didn't truly recognize as an automobile. Once we convinced her to *pretend* this was a car and pretend to be driving as though it was real, it appeared she was grasping the concept. She did, however, repeat her statement. "I don't know why I have to do this!" Her performance of the test was definitely under protest.

Beyond the windshield of this mock vehicle, there was a screen that displayed animated roads and streets moving as though you were driving, and the speed adjusted in coordination with the pedals. She was confused when the instructor told her to put her foot on the accelerator. Finally, I told Mom to put her foot on the gas pedal, and she complied.

Their conclusion was a recommendation that she give up driving. We honestly didn't feel she had done that poorly, especially under the circumstances. They put an old woman in a box and told her to drive. After explaining to them that she had limited her driving to daylight hours and familiar routes (no freeway) and we had been passengers with her and not disturbed by her driving, we were able to convince them to schedule an actual behind-the-wheel test for her. This will happen in a couple of weeks.

Karen and I don't like to talk about Mom or the testing in front of Mom. We waited until we had dropped her off and then began our recount of the day and shared our observations and opinions. We concluded that we feel defensive on Mom's behalf. We acknowledge the strain these appointments and tests put on Mom and are at a loss as how to ease that for her.

February, week 4 (eight weeks)

The follow-up visit with Dr. Miller was this week. When we picked Mom up, as usual, she was waiting in the lobby for us. I commented to Karen that Mom had on a different outfit. Karen informed me that she had told her the day before that she had to change, since she had worn the same garb a couple of days in a row.

Dr. Miller began the visit by asking Mom about the tests she had taken at the neurologist last week. Mom claimed she didn't remember taking any tests. We tried to stimulate her memory by reminding her where we had gone to lunch and where we had shopped after the visit. Nothing. How do you forget something just days after, especially when it caused so much irritation for you? I thought maybe she was being stubborn and refusing to answer because she didn't like the doctor. It appears that Karen and I are the only people she likes these days.

He proceeded to explain to us that her memory was very poor and diagnosed her with dementia. He supplied us with lots of reading material about the disease. We have homework.

March, week 1 (nine weeks)

Karen took Mom to have her hearing tested and reported it was just fine. I was really surprised. Apparently, her issue is not poor hearing; it's poor listening. Possibly it's attitudinal; she doesn't like what she's being asked or told, so she chooses not to respond.

Because of snow, we cancelled the driving test. Mom would not drive in these conditions, so it would be absurd to test her under these circumstances. We rescheduled for two weeks from now.

Mom is upset that she has to take this test at all and demands it be done in her car, the vehicle she's familiar with. I have explained several times why they have to use their car, mainly because it has dual controls. She's not buying it. I get so irritated with her; she just refuses to understand. Finally, I just quit explaining and gave her the choice, "Either you take the test or you give up your car. Those are your choices." I get so perturbed with her that my tone of voice is harsh and my volume is more than necessary (especially since I learned her hearing is just fine). I feel bad when I let my frustration show.

March, week 2 (ten weeks)

I made a surprise visit to Mom's this morning. It's a secured building, so I had to call her to let me in. She wouldn't press the button by her phone that gives visitors access; instead, she came down from the far end of the third floor to open the door. We went up to her apartment, and I showed her the button by the phone for letting people in. She stated that she couldn't figure it out. It's a button labeled "open." What's to figure out?

I couldn't help but notice that she has clothes hung on racks that she's attached to the outside of her foyer closet doors. The foyer is full of clothing. I asked her if she's run out of closet space. She "supposed" so.

I also noticed how filthy her kitchen floor was—I was sticking to it as I attempted to walk through—and commented on it. I learned my fastidious cleaning from her; this was out of the ordinary. Her response was that she has lots of things she should do.

She constantly complains that she's "bored." Next time she does that, I'll suggest she wash her kitchen floor.

I realized that it had been quite a while since I had actually been inside her apartment. She would always be waiting in the lobby when we picked her up. We hadn't gone up to her apartment in months. When I saw the disarray and grime, I surmised she must have not wanted us to see it. On the other hand, she seemed rather aloof to the mess.

March, week 3 (eleven weeks)

Driving test day! Mom met me in the lobby, and we waited for the instructor. She wasn't about to let this woman (the enemy) in her apartment. After seeing the condition of her place last week, I can understand and appreciate this tactic.

The two of them assumed their positions in the test vehicle and took off. I waited. About an hour later, they pulled back into the lot and emerged from the car. The body language of both spoke volumes; immediately, I knew it had not gone as well as I hoped. Silently they entered the lobby, Mom with a scowl on her face and Tricia, the instructor, looking shell-shocked. We got ourselves comfortable on the upholstered lobby chairs and began the dreaded conversation regarding the test. Tricia confessed she had actually experienced fear as the passenger. During the test, Mom, following Tricia's instruction, had made a turn taking her one block off the beaten trail and then became disoriented. She could not recover from this one turn, and they continued driving, Mom not recognizing any street names. Since Tricia was unfamiliar with the area, she could offer no suggestions as they ventured farther and farther away from their starting point. After several minutes, Mom recognized a store, realized she was heading the wrong direction, and managed to correct using a parking lot to turn around. The other issue Tricia had was with Mom's speed; she was too slow and refused to yield to vehicles who were reduced to tailgating her. That I could associate with. Mom will pick a lane and expect to stay in it for an entire journey. I actually think she accomplished that on a trip from Minneapolis to Milwaukee a few years back.

After lengthy discussion, my pointing out that she had observed all traffic laws and for the most part was aware of her task and reminding her of Mom's self-imposed restrictions, Tricia agreed to give her six months of restricted driving and then retest. I'm not sure if Mom understood she only had a limited time before a repeat of this day, but, for now, she savored her victory.

March, week 4 (twelve weeks)

Karen and I have been discussing what we've read about dementia. We're acknowledging some things that we noticed possibly even a year or more ago but didn't actually comprehend as a sign of the disease.

Not very long ago, we were very upset with Mom for not attending a funeral of a close friend of hers. We chastised her for choosing to go on a bingo outing with apartment cohorts rather than paying her respects to a dear friend of many years. Now I'm wondering if she chose not to attend the funeral for fear she wouldn't recognize people that she should know.

We've noticed how often she repeats the same statement, like small talk. It's the proverbial broken record, and it's irritating to us. We've complained to each other and shared how we react, which is oftentimes sarcastic or rude. Neither of us have much patience with her.

Mom often won't answer a question; she'll stare back at you in silence. I'll get annoyed with her and ask her in a stern voice why she won't answer me. Karen has also experienced this, and her reaction is similar to mine.

Karen thinks Mom can't read a menu any longer. She'll ask odd questions about menu items, asking what common menu items are and if we think she'd like them. She constantly wants to know what you're ordering, and then she'll order the same.

Mom's clothes are like uniforms. She wears the same outfits time after time. One Sunday, I remarked that she had a spill on her fleece sweater and she should wash it. She didn't know if it was washable and wanted me to look at the tag on the neck. I had seen her in this sweater no less than fifty times—I didn't want to touch the neck!

We're wondering if all these things are a result of the dementia.

We talked about how we find ourselves *handling* Mom and so often needing to issue correction like you would with a child. I don't like the feeling of parenting my mother. I'm not ready for this.

March, week 5 (thirteen weeks)

The neurologist suggested we make an appointment with a fellow on staff at the clinic who is an expert in dementia. I am learning a lot about dementia from the material given me at the clinic and from surfing the web, but I am willing to learn more.

I am having difficulty with patience in regard to Mom. I try but can't seem to maintain it very long and end up showing my aggravation with her; then I feel horrible. I would love to learn some tactics to maintain patience and actually appear to be a nice daughter more of the time.

I took Mom to do her taxes this week. For many years, she used to make an appointment and handle it on her own; but this year, she claimed she couldn't remember how to get there. She was very concerned that she didn't know what to bring with her, yet she had extremely organized files for every consideration.

During the session, she couldn't answer the preparer's question with anything other than "I don't know."

"Did you pay estimated tax this year?"

"I don't know."

"Did you make any other charitable contributions?"

"I don't know."

Exasperated, I firmly stated, through grit teeth, that answer just wasn't going to fly. I lost my patience yet again.

After Mom asked to use the tax preparer's restroom, she emerged and admitted she hadn't flushed because she couldn't figure it out. It was a button on the side rather than a handle, but I would think most everyone could have figured it out. I swear a monkey has more deductive reasoning than my mother.

April, week 1 (fourteen weeks)

This year, I have been picking Mom up for Sunday dinner and dominos at my house during the winter. Now that the weather has improved and the roads are clear, I thought she could drive over. She called to ask for directions. She's been making this Sunday ritual for over seven years, over 350 times, and she's forgotten the way to travel the three miles? I decided to pick her up. Maybe her driving career should be over.

At dinner, she actually asked, "What's that?" when I placed a baked potato on her plate. She seems amused with herself that she doesn't remember things, like it's a charming act she's performing. I don't find it entertaining in the least. Once on her plate, the potato remained untouched until I dressed it for her. She seemed not to know what to do with it. I have difficulty believing she doesn't know what to do with a potato; she seems to like the added attention of me fixing her plate.

She recently bought herself a cane, claiming she needs it for stability. It's like a prop to her. She doesn't use it at all in the house, parks it in a corner until someone comes over, and then she retrieves it, places it next to her, and announces that now she needs a cane. This is another example of why I think so much of her exploits are an act. It appears to me that she's seeking attention.

After dinner, we played our usual game of Mexican Train Dominos, and she is perfection at the game. She employs strategy and often wins. I can't figure out how she can count and add and play this game with such fervor, yet she doesn't recognize a potato! I just don't get it. I had understood that the comprehension of numbers was one of the first concepts to go with Alzheimer's. Of course, my mother would be the exception; she lost the ability to recognize vegetables.

April, week 2 (fifteen weeks)

Mom wanted to put a few dollars in envelopes for the kids for Easter. She had trouble recalling which great-grandchild went with which grandchild. She claims that it's difficult to remember the children when you don't see them often. She had seen them all a few months back at Christmas. I made her a list, a mini family tree, to keep with her appointment calendar. She placed the list in the calendar, right next to the one she already had written for herself.

I have a wonderful friend who is going through this with her mother and shares stories with me of her experiences. Her mother seems to be further along with the disease, so Debra has encountered most all of the things that are new to me. She doesn't have much sympathy for my impatience and sense of irritability with Mom. There just seems to be so many contradictions in Mom's behavior and memory. It's like I really don't believe her when she so quickly and eagerly states, "I don't remember," as though she's proud of that fact.

I asked Mom about a dish she used to make when we were kids because I wanted to make it for Easter. Her response was "I forgot how to cook." Really?

I know I'm just not *getting* it. I argue with Debra that my mother's actions are attention seeking and not because of dementia. Debra disagrees.

April, week 3 (sixteen weeks)

Spring is here, and the snow is gone. I'm feeling somewhat sad because I didn't get my annual Vegas trip with Mom this year. To mentally and emotionally survive a Minnesota winter, I like to get away to a warmer climate in February, or March by the latest, for at least a few days. I decided last year was the final trip to Vegas with Mom; it had just become too difficult, not to mention she made a comment of "I just can't do this anymore" before we were even out of the airport. I couldn't imagine what was so trying for her.

I learned on that trip that she had acquired a fear of escalators. This was new to me. I discovered this as I stood at the bottom of one (I thought she was right behind me) and she was at the top, yelling, "I can't do it! I can't do it!" A nice young fellow assisted her, while I, the insensitive, apparently noncaring daughter, waited at the bottom. We had to look around to find elevators from that point on. I asked her when she acquired this fear. It was no surprise that her answer was "I don't know."

For years, prior to a Vegas trip, we practiced playing blackjack and even memorized the basic strategy. On the airplane, we would test each other on what would be the appropriate action if certain cards were dealt. We knew the game. We enjoyed playing. This particular trip, as we sat down at a table to play blackjack, Mom was shocked to learn she needed to purchase chips with which to place a bet. I remember thinking that she was acting silly and trying to be funny. It didn't dawn on me that she didn't remember the process.

It was a variety of things that occurred on that trip that made me realize she really didn't want to take trips any longer. She wasn't enjoying the time away; she appeared stressed by it. The entire episode was frustrating for me; it was like traveling with a toddler.

April, week 4 (seventeen weeks)

The manager of Mom's building called and suggested we consider moving Mom to an assisted-living facility. He said that they just couldn't provide the care she needed. Her apartment building is all seniors, and he explained that they observe their tenants for changes and will contact the family when they notice a pattern of strange behavior or suspect they are not eating. He mentioned a few things, but the biggest issue was an episode where Mom had soiled her sofa and asked for his assistance to cover it with a blanket. He told me the sofa needed to be cleaned, not covered. Mom didn't understand that. He had been invited into her unit, and I'm certain he also noticed the dirty floors and the clothes hanging in the foyer. There were also stacks of mail, receipts and scraps of paper covering the counter and table, and shopping bags stuffed into every crevice. There was a heavy coating of dust on everything.

What I gathered was this is a suggestion, not an order of eviction. It definitely is something to think about.

When I informed Karen of this call, she told me that Mom's hairdresser had mentioned to her that they were concerned for Mom. They had noticed some changes in her.

Are we not seeing these changes because we don't want to?

May, week 1 (eighteen weeks)

Karen and I decided to approach Mom about having us be appointed power of attorney and having access and signing privileges on her accounts. We were surprised when she seemed agreeable. Because of the issues I had experienced with the tax preparation and a recommendation of the tax preparer, I felt it was time to step up and protect Mom's finances. She has, up to now, been secretive about her finances and actually seemed to be distrustful of us, though undeserved. So we were shocked yet relieved that she was willing to take this step.

Since we began traveling together about twenty years ago, we noticed how attached to her purse Mom was. In the motel room at night, she kept it near the bed, up by her head. I figured she was keeping it safe from a possible intruder intending to rob us. Heck, if someone broke into our room for our purses, I'd be throwing mine at him—"Take it. Don't hurt me." Then we began to wonder if she was keeping it away from us, fearful we might rifle through it while she slept. Mom was not one to trust others, even family. I think she learned that from Grandma.

Mom never talked money to us. We never knew how much she earned or how much she had saved or invested. All we did know is that she was frugal and kept detailed records of every expenditure she made, down to the penny. We assumed she had wealth but were never privy to the details. Once allowed knowledge, our curiosity and assumptions of prosperity proved to be correct. Mom invested well and managed her personal finances in an exemplary fashion.

Mom had been an employee of the bank since I was in junior high school. Prior to that, she had been a stay-at-home-mom. From teller to bank officer, Mom excelled at her job. She took classes and listened to self-help tapes. She knew her business. She obviously paid attention and utilized much of what she learned with her personal finances. Shorty after Mom retired, she went back to work in the operations center of the bank, advancing to the position of lead after a couple of years. She retired for good after her eighty-third birthday, dreading the winter commute; or so she claimed. We were beginning to wonder if her lapses of memory were affecting her work.

Mom will still have control of her banking, but as this disease progresses, we will be able to take over at some point.

May, week 2 (nineteen weeks)

Another suggestion from the neurologist was to organize a weekly pill box for Mom. I picked up two pill organizers with morning and evening compartments for each day of the week and went over to Mom's apartment to accomplish this mission. I was unprepared for the battle that ensued. Her pills, prescriptions and vitamins, were mostly in the kitchen cupboard, with random bottles here and there on the counter. She literally grabbed bottles out of my hands, saying, "Not that one!" Several times I calmly explained why this was a good idea. She was so frantic that I was handling her things, she couldn't listen; she was too focused on the bottles. About the sixth time explaining the concept, I totally lost it. I found myself yelling the reason; people on the first floor could hear me! Then I burst into tears and told her I was trying to help her and the doctor had instructed me to use the pill boxes.

The crying made her pause and, finally, begrudgingly conform. I accomplished filling one box. I had regained my composure and attempted the instruction portion of this endeavor. I told her to open the lid for the appropriate day and time and take the pills and to ignore the bottles. I would come over weekly and refill the box.

I was exhausted when I left Mom's. I was exhausted and annoyed with myself for letting her get to me. I didn't enjoy yelling at her. Volume isn't going to make her understand better. I need to find a better way to cope.

May, week 3 (twenty weeks)

I headed over to Mom's to refill the pill box. I found it hadn't been touched; all the pills remained intact in all the little sections. I questioned her about it, and her response was "Oh, I don't use that thing." I did not want a repeat of last week. I explained one more time why she should use the pill box, doubting it would have any impact. I contemplated taking the prescription bottles with me, but anticipating a knock-down-drag-out fight, I reconsidered. I also feared she wouldn't take any pills if she didn't have the bottles.

There was a doctor visit not all that long ago where they adjusted her high blood pressure medication because her blood pressure had gotten too low. Now I'm beginning to wonder if she may have forgotten she had taken a pill and then took it again. I wish she'd let me control the pills. Having her responsible for her own medication could be deadly.

While in her apartment, she showed me a letter she had gotten from the IRS that she didn't understand. The letter explained she had paid an overage on her taxes. The difference was the amount of the estimated tax that she claimed she had not paid. Obviously, she had in fact paid it but forgot. I noticed that the bottom third of the letter had been torn off. I asked where the rest of the letter was, but she couldn't remember. I told her it was a letter of information and no action was required. I suggested she keep it with her tax papers; at which point, she placed it on the top of one of the many piles on her counter. I asked, "Mom, don't you have a file for your tax papers?" She answered, "Probably."

I guess it might be time to check out assisted living.

May, week 4 (twenty-one weeks)

I took a half day off from work to bring Mom to an early afternoon appointment with the dementia specialist. She's fatigued with all these trips to the doctor and complains the entire car ride. I'm getting exhausted too, and Mom's constant complaining doesn't help. She does not want to participate in any more tests. The only way to appease her is to suggest stopping for a treat after the clinic. This idea calmed her for a while.

The specialist seemed rushed, almost as though he was in a panic. It was somewhat unnerving. Almost immediately, he separated Mom from me. He left her with an assistant to assess her using another Mini-Mental test. Oh, joy! Another test! I feared Mom would pull her annoyance routine and refuse to answer or, worse, purposely answer incorrectly. She doesn't grasp how important these tests are.

The specialist and I talked for a short time, and he asked me about my concerns for Mom. I mentioned her wearing the same clothes repeatedly and that I suspected she didn't bathe. He basically responded that those things were not important. After about a half hour, I had been told at least four times his three rules: "you can't argue with her," "you can't force her," and "let her have her way." My question was "What if what she's doing is harmful for her?" thinking about her medications. He repeated, "You can't argue with her, you can't force her, and let her have her way." I muttered, "You obviously don't have children." I guess I pressed a button because he became quite animated and very intensely stated, "That's not germane to this conversation!" I wanted so badly to respond, "Well, then, which one is it? Janet, Michael, or Tito?"

I like to think I approached this appointment with an open mind. I have been reading and trying to absorb all I can, educating myself to this disease. What I really needed was some advice on how to handle some of the situations that arise. I wanted some tools. I desired to learn how to maintain patience. Instead, I got a lecture. I got "You can't, you can't, you can't . . ." So what *can* I do? I was so disillusioned by this session that I was not curious in the least what session number two would entail.

When Mom and I were finally reunited at the end of the appointment, I could sense she was upset. I queried how it went for her, and she responded that she didn't like *that man*. I asked why, but she couldn't explain. She said she didn't want to come back. I agreed with her and promised her we wouldn't have to, adding, "Let's go get a piece of pie!" Her demeanor immediately changed; she had a new focus.

We went to a restaurant known for their pies, not far from her apartment. She wolfed down her slice like she was in a pie-eating contest. I tried to savor my slice and engage in some conversation at the same time. I think I realized where I had learned my impatience from; Mom was done eating, so, as far as she was concerned, it was time for the check. My phone rang, and it was a call I was waiting for from work. I needed to take the call to handle a time-sensitive issue. Before I knew it, Mom was up from her chair, looking for the waitress. I tried to grab her arm, but she had already moved beyond my reach. Our table was near the kitchen, and Mom walked right in there in search of the waitress with our bill. I jumped up and ran to retrieve Mom from an area customers are not allowed into. I firmly grabbed her arm to pull her from the kitchen. She immediately began yelling, "Ouch, ouch!" I hadn't grabbed her hard enough to inflict pain. The restaurant went quiet, and I felt everyone's eyes on us. I directed Mom back to the table and pointed at the chair, indicating she should sit. I quickly concluded my phone conversation and then addressed her calmly, saying, "You can't go in the kitchen." She sat looking very displeased while I finished my piece of pie. The manager of the restaurant approached our table and asked, "Is everything all right?" I responded, "Yes, the pie is delicious."

June, week 1 (twenty-two weeks)

Karen and I invited Mom out to lunch. She seemed excited with the idea, since it had been some time since the three of us had done anything fun together that didn't involve a clinic. The truth is it was lunch at Jamestown Estate, an assisted-living facility that we wanted to check out. We had made an appointment for a tour. Once there, Mom figured it out and was not pleased. Yes, we tricked her. We felt she would never agree to look into it; deceiving her was our only option.

The housing director joined us for lunch, but Mom refused to engage in conversation. It was a lovely, very tasty lunch in a beautifully decorated dining room. Karen mentioned the room reminded her of a cruise ship dining room. The meal, selected from a menu of three choices, was presented very nicely, served on a linen table cloth with linen napkins. The waitstaff was uniformed and professional (though Mom was her new-normal rude with them).

After lunch, we took a tour of the facility, including a one-bedroom unit that was available. It had a bay window with a view of the gardens and walking path below. Mom tried her best to appear unimpressed. Finally, she said that she couldn't afford it. I corrected her. I've seen her portfolio; she could afford it. She seemed to be verging on a panic attack and needed to sit down. I took her hand and told her that she had worked and saved all her life; it was time to spend some of it on herself. This was a classy place for a classy lady. She deserved it; it was time to be a "princess."

We wanted so badly for this to be her decision and not because of being forced out of her home. She repeated that she couldn't afford it and added that she only received a thousand dollars a month. I really don't know where she got that figure, but it was way off. I took the chance to correct her, and she seemed surprised but accepted what I told her as truth. She could afford this apartment.

We signed the papers that day and left a deposit. Whew!

June, week 2 (twenty-three weeks)

We have only a month to get her packed and out of the apartment. We are facing the daunting chore of going through the accumulation of things spanning thirty years. The new apartment at Jamestown Estate is smaller with no storage room, so we will have to downsize a lot. Trying to be organized in our approach, we figure we will mark boxes to move, boxes to throw, and boxes to donate or sell in a garage sale. Her place is extremely cluttered, which makes it difficult to work. Our first project will be clearing off the counters and tables to give us some space to work.

Mom understands she's moving but clearly doesn't like the two of us rummaging through her things. She finds it hard to be overseeing both of our activities at the same time. She got somewhat disturbed when we moved all her piles of papers and things from the counter. We explain every motion we make. Karen found a box of old papers, bank statements, and paid bills, and assigned Mom the job of shredding them. This keeps her busy and distracted from what we are up to.

We have a cart that we fill with papers and magazines for recycle. Mom can't stand it when it's half full and insists on bringing it down to the trash area in the garage. This is often a twice-a-day process, but at least she gets some exercise and a break from shredding. She never takes her cane with her, but we don't point that out to her.

We're trying to be sensitive in regard to her belongings. We don't want to randomly toss something out if it holds some sentimental value to Mom, so we ask, "Do you want to keep this?" to which she responds nine out of ten times, "Do you want it?" Then comes our explanation about the move and that she can take anything with her that she wants. We're not going through her stuff because we want things; she's moving *with* the things she wants. This goes on several times a day. Now *we've* become the broken record.

Working together toward the goal of moving Mom provides a boost in the area of patience for both Karen and me. When feeling frustrated, we can look at the other and do the eye-rolling thing, and it seems to help.

June, week 3 (twenty-four weeks)

We've been over to Mom's every day this week. We feel like we've made more of a mess than progress. Partly what thwarts our forward movement is that Mom unpacks things at night that we've packed during the day. I had the top of her dresser cleared off the other day, and when I returned, there it was, all set back up. She's really quite agreeable when you remind her we're packing to move and that we'd really appreciate if she'd leave the things in the boxes. But then she forgets, and back in their assigned places go the knickknacks.

We may have to fill the boxes and take them with us to avoid repacking daily. I feel sympathy for Mom. Each evening, her apartment doesn't look like her place, and it must make her uncomfortable. With our time limit, we can't do much about that situation.

We've narrowed Mom's collections down. Her Kewpies are displayed in a wall curio, so they will be easy to move. Her angels are going with her; many of them were gifts from the grandkids, but the Betty Boop collection will be sold. Mom had the final decision on what she wanted to keep. She was quite agreeable to our suggestions.

In our breaks between sorting and packing, Karen and I have been talking about the probability of taking Mom's car away. Karen told me that Mom got lost the other week. She was forced to make a turn because of some road construction and suddenly didn't recognize the area. She drove for nearly two hours before identifying a building in a nearby suburb. She was five minutes away from her home, driving in circles for the two hours. Mom thought it was funny; we didn't.

June, week 4 (twenty-five weeks)

Our packing is often interrupted by moments of amusement at what we find. Karen brought a brand-new bottle of glue to my attention. Clearly on the label was printed "White Glue." It was brown. I never knew glue had an expiration date.

I found a spice container of cinnamon from Red Owl. That store has been out of business for twenty years or more. There were unopened tins of hard candy from a store that went belly-up ten years ago. I can't believe the amount of trash we've generated.

I found a drawer full of granola bars. Boxes and boxes of bars, opened with one taken out of each. I started to read expiration dates and found some as old as three years. The drawer under that was filled with rolls of waxed paper, sandwich bags, and cellophane wrap. The three of us will not have to buy any of those products for years!

We're also finding boxes of brand-new items, in multiples. There were static dusters, six of them, and squeegees, again a half dozen. Why would anyone need that many dusters and squeegees unless you were running a cleaning business with several employees? Then there was a bag of two dozen new pens that, according to the packing slip, she had paid nearly thirty dollars for. She could have bought the equivalent at the dollar store for three dollars. With some investigation, we discovered she's been getting "prize award" notifications from several different places, and most are accompanied with offers to purchase things—like squeegees and static dusters. It seems like she thinks she must pay this "bill," and then these things arrive a week or so later. When confronted with this, she promised to quit doing it. These businesses have found a gold mine with the geriatric community! Hopefully now they'll have one less with whom to take advantage.

June, week 5 (twenty-six weeks)

Moving day will be this coming weekend. We will have this place another month after that to clean and clear out the rest of the stuff not making the move. Fortunately, the building owner is replacing carpeting and appliances, so we do not have to clean those.

I've been focusing on the kitchen and storage room. Karen's been working on the bathroom, bedroom, and closet. We're still producing boxes and bags of trash daily. Karen trimmed down the shoe collection from about forty pairs to a sensible dozen. I discovered a box full of magazines dating back to 1968. That means that particular box made the move to this apartment over thirty years ago. Its final destination is the recycle bin in the garage.

Karen has filled her trunk a couple of times with garbage bags full of clothes to donate to charity. Some of the items still have price tags on them. She found one pantsuit circa 1960 that had a neck and cuffs of marabou. I can't imagine when Mom would have worn this hideous garment.

We decided this would be the right time to tell her she can't take her car with her. Debra told me about "creative lying." We told Mom she's not allowed to have a car at Jamestown Estate and that they will drive her wherever she needs to go, or one of us will drive her. We'll top that off with a sad story about how one of the grandkids needs a car. So much for the plan, we met with one of the nurses at the new place to assess Mom's needs, with Mom in attendance. Suddenly, Mom loudly announced, "I don't know why I can't have my car here!" The nurse answered that she didn't see why she couldn't. Well, thank you very much! I wish the nurse had said something vague, like she would check it out, and then privately talk with one of us to see what the story was. We made up a tale for Mom (more creative lying) that she would have to pay a ridiculous amount for a garage. Between that and urging her to give her car to one of the grandsons, we got her back on track.

July, week 1 (twenty-seven weeks)

A couple of days before the move, we went to the new place to sign some paperwork. One of the items we wanted to complete was the living will. The facility needed to have this on file before she moved in. Mom is cognitive enough to make such decisions, though she continually asked me what I would do. I told her the truth. There would be no extreme lifesaving efforts made.

On the day of the move, before we drove her to Jamestown Estate, Mom handed over her car keys without too much argument. We reminded her that she had agreed to this, and since she didn't remember, she trusted we were telling the truth. All in all, it went pretty well.

We completed the marathon move in one day. Husbands and kids helped. We got Mom involved in an activity with the other residents at the new place to keep her out from underfoot. She likes playing card games and being social. She joined right in and appeared to be having a good time. It looks like this will be a good fit for her.

The new apartment is cozy yet bright with a big bay window. It has a small kitchen, but the gas stove has been disabled. There's a microwave and a decent-size refrigerator, which we filled with soda, cranberry juice, cheese, and yogurt. The bedroom is spacious with a huge walk-in closet. The dining set and small curio fit nicely in the dining room, but the living room is smaller, so we opted to keep the love seat and abandon the matching sofa.

All Mom's familiar things are displayed in all the right places to make it look familiar. The major difference from this place to her old apartment is the lack of clutter.

Her mirrors are spaced by a minimum of ten-foot intervals and adorn every room. Her clocks are all set to the correct time and visible from every angle in every room. We positioned her upholstered rocker in front of the TV with the end table next to it housing her favorite Word-Find puzzle books and pens. This is home.

July, week 2 (twenty-eight weeks)

Karen visited Mom early in the morning the day after the move to be certain she survived her first night without incident. She told me that Mom hugged her hard, a genuine hug, which is something she seldom did. Jamestown Estate is three blocks from her old apartment, yet Mom seemed to think she was many miles away, possibly in the next state. She must have felt we deserted her and was frightened, feeling alone. That made me feel sad.

Mom was so happy to see Karen but seemed to struggle with the idea that she didn't live far away. Karen assured her she lived close by and she would be returning soon. We had a few small boxes and items at the old place that we needed to bring over, so we left Mom in the rotunda with her puzzle book.

Karen and I stopped by a little later and found Mom in the dining room contentedly sipping coffee with four other ladies. She was happy to see us and accompanied us up to her new digs so we could unpack the last couple of boxes. She appeared to have gotten beyond the initial fear she awoke with. She almost seemed happy.

This was the perfect time to switch to a pill box; all medications will be administered by the nursing staff at the facility. I told Mom it was a rule of this place (actually, we are paying extra to include this service). She knows it's assisted living, and that's somewhat difficult for her to agree to. She's been independent for so many years. We keep trying to encourage her by telling her that it's all right, she's gotten older, and needing a little help is fine and normal. On the plus side to this assisted-living facility, there are lots of activities and lots of opportunity to socialize—her forte.

Once we got her set up with a group activity, we headed back to the old apartment to work on getting it ready to totally vacate. My current project is to clean out the refrigerator. Even though they are replacing it, I don't want to leave it a mess. I also planned to wipe out the cupboards, especially the one where I found an exploded can of pineapple (it probably had made the thirty-year previous move). It most likely exploded years ago; the "juice" had become like epoxy, and the remnants of the can had to be pried out.

From the refrigerator, I discarded a block of cream cheese that had expired five years ago. There were also several restaurant containers from who knows when or where. I resisted sniffing anything for fear of permanent damage to my nasal passages.

July, week 3 (twenty-nine weeks)

Hopefully I have made the last trip to the garbage cans in the garage of the old place. This trip included a six-pack of beverage that I had, at a glance, thought to be iced tea. It turned out to be orange juice, brown orange juice.

I found a jar packed full of the cotton from the tops of aspirin bottles; many years' worth of cotton. I wonder what she had intended to do with it. I found name tag badges from every event she had ever attended. Earlier, as I was finding them in every drawer, Mom was forcing me to shred them to protect herself from identify theft. I had tried to explain it was just her name on them, no social security number or any other number for that fact, just her name. I realized this was the "you can't argue with her" rule. This last batch, however, is not being shredded; it is going intact into the garbage. Anarchy!

Karen and I got hungry from our working and discovered a package of cookies. Refusing to read the expiration date, we opened it and discovered the cookies were crisp deliciousness. We ate our fill, not wanting to know how old they were, and washed them down with bottled water Karen had brought with her.

Even after a month of Mom of shredding papers, there were still a couple of boxes left. I decided to bring them home to look through in my leisure. I haven't had leisure time in months; I wonder what it feels like.

July, week 4 (thirty weeks)

Well, that's it; I turned in the keys to the old apartment. We will pay them to discard the sofa and a cardboard armoire. Other than those two items, the place is empty and clean.

Mom seems to have settled in to her new place. She doesn't remember the names of the people she dines with, three meals a day, or the people she plays games with, but no one seems to mind.

Even though I bought her a small desk, she uses her dining room table as a workstation for paying bills and storing paperwork. Among these papers were three months of bank statements, so I offered to balance her checkbook. She still maintains her own finances, but it seems to cause her tension. Though resistant, she finally agreed to allow me to reconcile her checking account. Even though it was three months' worth of statements, it wasn't difficult because she doesn't have many bills. The confusing things were a check written to the IRS and an additional deposit from them. The notice she received a few months back was making her aware of the actual figures of what she owed in taxes for the previous year, with no action required. She interpreted it as a bill and promptly wrote them out a check. They, in turn, had to refund that. Now I know what happened to the bottom third of the letter. She used it like a payment coupon when she submitted the check. It may be time to take over her checkbook.

August, week 1 (thirty-one weeks)

I need to learn the nuances of living in and visiting an assisted-living facility. I made a major discovery this week; when leaving the building, you do not hold the door open for people.

There's a screened-in porch just beyond the entryway, and some residents sit in the rockers or padded chairs and enjoy the scenery and fresh air. I was taking Mom to the store, and as we were leaving, a gentleman in a wheelchair was struggling to catch the door that led to the porch. Being the accommodating person that I am, I held the door open so he could maneuver his chair through it. As his feet passed the door jam, an ear-piercing alarm sounded. Immediately, I surmised he wasn't allowed outdoors; he must have been on house arrest. I attempted to position myself in front of him, but he kept coming. I had my hands on the arms of his chair, facing him and trying to stand my ground, but finding myself being pushed backward through the doorway. I nearly lost my balance and landed in his lap as I'm trying very politely and calmly to point out to him that I didn't think he was supposed to be leaving. My rescuer was a spindly woman in a smock who came running from the lobby, loudly ordering, "Ralph, you know you can't go out there!" She basically ignored me, for which I was thankful.

August, week 2 (thirty-two weeks)

I wonder if I will get used to conversations with old people in an assisted-living building. I try to be pleasant and cordial, but, apparently, many of them have lost their filters. They appear to be affable too, but then they speak and pretty much say what they think.

Today, I was walking through the rotunda looking for Mom, and a very large woman in a muumuu decided to direct me to where she was. I acknowledged her, and she offered, "Your mother always looks so nice." I thanked her for her observation, but then she added, "The mother looks better than the daughter." Shocked, I awkwardly laughed and said, "Yes, I suppose she does." My snap decision to not kick a woman in a wheelchair in the shins was probably a wise one.

Once in Mom's apartment, I took advantage of viewing myself in one of her many mirrors to see if I had forgotten part of my makeup or had made a poor choice of clothing that morning. I thought I looked fairly decent. I think I will avoid that muumuu-wearing woman in the future.

August, week 3 (thirty-three weeks)

I went to join Mom for lunch at Jamestown Estate. From the foyer, I noticed Ralph eying the door, so I made a quick entrance once I was buzzed in. I veered a sharp left to avoid muumuu-wearing lady. I made it to the elevator unscathed. Once in Mom's apartment, I found her upset that she couldn't find her cane. She had no idea where she had left it. I suggested we go down to the desk and ask if anyone found it. Sure enough, she had left it behind after a card game. That proves my point; if you *need* something, like she claims, you don't mislay it. She walks all around the place with no assistance until she realizes she has no cane, and then she's crippled. I will not, however, argue the point with her. I am learning.

I have memorized the names of the four ladies who dine with Mom. When I join them, I usually sit to Mom's left with Marie on my left. Next to Marie sits Jane and then Esther and Priscilla completing the circle on Mom's right. Marie is the talkative one. I'm not certain if Jane can speak; she may have suffered a stroke. Esther is definitely hard of hearing, and Priscilla seems to be quiet by nature.

A menu on the table lists the choices for the particular meal. Each person sits in their assigned seat where a glass of juice awaits them. The staff has already learned that Mom's juice of choice is cranberry. The ladies look over the menu to select one of three items offered. The waitstaff is there to take orders within seconds of the table being filled; they are friendly and helpful and speak loudly. Mom orders whatever I order. It makes me wonder what she eats on the days I don't join her (probably whatever Marie is ordering).

Priscilla is the table's dump station. Whatever anyone doesn't feel like eating, they offer to Priscilla. I think she ate an entire bag of chips at this meal. Her daughter commented to me last week that Priscilla has been gaining weight even though the doctor has urged her to lose some. I wonder if I should tell Priscilla's daughter I have figured out why.

August, week 4 (thirty-four weeks)

When we moved Mom into the new apartment, we were thrilled to find a very large walk-in closet in her bedroom. This woman has clothes! After we had thrown away worn-out slacks, she still had fifty-seven pairs. I forced her to select the best of the best to make the move with her. We narrowed it down to about twenty. It's the same story with shoes; we got rid of all the stilettos and worn-out pairs, but she still had enough to line the three walls of the closet. I have noticed recently that the shoes have found their way out of the closet and now line her bedroom walls.

I have developed a theory; on good days, she understands the concept of a closet. On a bad day, that door is just a part of the wall. On a good day, she opens the door and selects one of the twenty pairs of slacks and a matching top. On a bad day, she only owns that outfit she hung on the hanger on her doorknob the night before. If the bad days double up, she may wear the same outfit three days in a row. However, she wears different shoes!

September, week 1
(thirty-five weeks)

Mom asks about her car. She admits to being dismayed that she can't simply take off when she wants. I offered to drive her where she wanted to go, but she couldn't think of any place.

In the past year, I would make it a point to call Mom a couple of times a week, and I would always ask how she was doing. Most times her answer was that she was bored. I would respond that "boredom is a choice." I didn't like hearing that complaint, sometimes feeling like I was being blamed for not entertaining her. All my life I never witnessed Mom being idle. She was constantly busy with a project, never bored. She was driven to make everything special, from a simple weekday dinner to a birthday party. I was so proud of my mother and imagined all my friends envied me because I had the best mother. I recall once a childhood friend stated to me that the only reason I was invited to all the birthday parties was because of the gift I gave. Mom would crochet a dress for an inexpensive plastic doll (pre-Barbie era). At the time, I didn't realize her efforts were probably due to the fact that money was short. The dolls were a hit; everyone wanted one, so Mom crocheted dress after dress. I figured my friend suffered some degree of jealousy, which led to her hurtful comment. I never told Mom about the incident.

Mom seems to be happy to have things to do with other residents in her new place. In the senior building she used to live in, according to the building manager, she had reduced herself to sitting in the lobby, working on Word-Find puzzles. She would wait for people to check their mailboxes or enter from the parking garage so she could greet them. This had apparently become a daily activity. There was a party room where residents gathered daily to socialize and play games. The manager told me that the residents had grown impatient with her for being slow. I wonder if she didn't quite understand the game or had forgotten how to play and appeared slow when she was, in reality, confused. I also wonder if she began to avoid the party room if people had shown their annoyance with her. Well, now she has easy card games and bingo and movie nights complete with popcorn. At least monthly, some form of entertainment is brought in for the residents to enjoy. Most recently, a fellow with a fiddle entertained them for a full hour one afternoon. Mom loved it!

I'm happy she's not sitting alone with a puzzle book. I'm also happy she's no longer complaining of being bored.

September, week 2
(thirty-six weeks)

Often, when I visit, I will find Mom in a chair in the rotunda working her Word-Find puzzles. If there's no activity going on at the moment, she will occupy herself with her puzzles. All of the chairs in the area are usually occupied, but very few people are socializing; mostly they're napping or staring off into space. Then there's Mom working on her puzzle book.

Wherever she goes, Mom carries a purse that houses her puzzle book, a couple of pencils, and her wallet. She insists on having money on her at all times. She prefers to have in excess of $200. This makes me and Karen very nervous, though her purse is never out of her sight, which is a good thing. I'd worry if she attached her money to her cane—that she loses all the time! I just don't like her having so much money on her. She is able to ride the courtesy van for errands, including the bank. Since she has control of her finances, we can't stop her from making withdrawals. I've tried to explain to her she doesn't need so much money, but again, it's an argument she won't let me win.

I still help her with bills; I write the checks, and she signs them. She's agreeable with that, but I would like to take the checkbook over altogether. I may take it with me, claiming I'm balancing it, and then just not return it, hoping she won't notice.

September, week 3
(thirty-seven weeks)

I visited Mom today and noticed that no matter where we went, Ralph was close behind in his wheelchair. I decided to test his resolve and made turns and zigzags, and Ralph was right on Mom's heels. Once I even did an about-face, yet he recovered in seconds. He mumbles something directed at Mom and has these big doe eyes and sweet smile. I leaned into Mom and whispered to her, "You're being followed." She responded in an exasperated tone, "I know! I can't stand that guy!" I wonder if Ralph thinks she's his wife. We ended up going into her apartment to escape him.

Checking out the bills she had on her table, I noticed Mom had a calendar of the current month's events and another of the week's menus on her desk. Looking them over, I remarked that I was going to have to make a point to join her for dinner on liver and onions night. She responded, "I'm really glad you found this place for me. I really like it here." Even with Ralph pursuing her, she likes it there.

Life is good.

September, week 4 (thirty-eight weeks)

I sat with Mom in the rotunda waiting for the dining room to open. She was more anxious than usual and kept asking the same question over and over. In an attempt to shift the focus, I noticed a woman in a motorized wheelchair and commented to her, "Nice ride." She stopped and showed me a few features on the unit and then introduced herself. In like manner, I introduced the two of us. "This is my mother, Louise, and I'm Maggie." She responded, "Maggie is a good name for a cow," and went on to describe her childhood farm and her sister who had a pet calf . . . I quit listening. I'm now up to avoiding Ralph and muumuu-wearing lady and have added motorized-wheelchair woman to my list.

I said (lied), "Nice to meet you," and suggested to Mom that we move closer to the dining room. They don't open the room for dinner until the stroke of four thirty. People have begun to surround the area as early as four o'clock, maybe even three. There seems to be a pecking order, an unwritten rule to allow the wheelchair users to be the front line. Behind them, the walker users sit or stand. If you have a cane, you take up the rear. Unless you're my mother, then you weasel your way through the crowd and stand directly in front of the entry. Still reeling from my cow name episode, I was not thinking clearly and closely followed her, excusing myself to each resident. "Excuse me. Pardon me. Excuse me." I don't know why I followed her so closely; I wasn't tethered to her. There I stood next to Mom; I would be second to enter the dining room. Since it's assigned seating, what is the point of being the first in?

The residents are like the geriatric version of Black Friday shoppers. I suspect some may camp out all night waiting for breakfast. They wait and don't converse; some nod off or otherwise occupy themselves; they simply stare at the empty dining room. The waitstaff, behind the invisible barrier, continues to set tables and place pitchers and menus. At exactly four thirty, the staff backs out of the way, and the checkered flag is dropped (figuratively). The lobby is cleared in no more than sixty seconds. It's pretty amazing. I've decided that next time I join Mom for a meal, I will just let her enjoy her "me first" attitude, and I'll hang behind. I'm realizing that I'm not responsible for her actions, only mine.

September, week 5
(thirty-nine weeks)

Jamestown Estate offered a flu shot clinic right there in the building for the first week in October. I signed Mom up for an appointment and gave her the reminder slip with the time and date. The condensed version of the ensuing conversation is as follows:

I made an appointment for you.
An appointment for what?
A flu shot.
Where?
Here.
When?
In two weeks. The date is on the slip.
Where will I go?
Come down to this area.
What time?
10:00 a.m.
For what?
A flu shot.
Where?
Here.

What time?
10:00 a.m.
Where do I go?

For the real-time version, just repeat the above eighteen times.

October, week 1 (forty weeks)

I stopped by Mom's place today and found Ralph *outside!* I had the urge to grab his wheelchair and rush him back inside, but I thought that may unnerve the younger woman who was sitting and chatting with him. When I got inside, I saw another fellow who could have been Ralph. This confused me. I guess I'll have to make them show me their ankles before I hold a door open for either one.

I found Mom having her nails done in the parlor. Weekly manicures and hair salon appointments; surely, this is heaven for Mom. When the manicure was done, after she forced the poor aide to retouch a couple of nails three times, we ran to the drugstore to pick up something she claimed she needed for her face. She said it came in a bottle, and when you pressed the top, white stuff came out. She even gave that exact description to the clerk. She couldn't tell us a brand or what purpose it served. We left empty-handed, since she wouldn't buy the refrigerated whipped cream topping that I suggested.

When I dropped her off, she commented, "I really like it here!" This is a comment I don't mind hearing her repeat.

October, week 2 (forty-one weeks)

I found Mom asleep in the rotunda this morning. This is not one of her better days. She's not able to recall things even thirty seconds later. She did, however, remember it was my birthday. She couldn't remember how old I was, so she asked, and I answered. Two minutes later, she asked again.

Mom showed me her list of needs, so I ended up taking her to the store for toothpaste even though she had bought a tube last week. She can't find it and insists she didn't buy it. On the way to the store, she asked two more times how old I was. When we got to the store, she wanted to know why we were there, so I answered, "For toothpaste, and I'm sixty-two years old." She bought her toothpaste, and we headed to the car. Before she would get in the car, she wanted to know if we had remembered the toothpaste (it was the only item we bought). On the way back to her place, she asked twice again how old I was. I'm old enough and vain enough to want to ignore the number!

This time, I brought her to her apartment, and we put the toothpaste in the vanity. By now, it was nearing one o'clock and a card bingo event, so she was anxious for me to depart. That was fine by me, since even short visits tend to exhaust me.

October, week 3 (forty-two weeks)

Mom's confusion turned out to be a symptom of a bladder infection. It was quite severe and landed her in the hospital. An untreated bladder infection can be deadly.

This is another lesson learned; confusion can be an indication of a urinary tract infection. We simply assumed her confusion was the progression of the disease. We didn't realize she was suffering from urgent and frequent urination, or pain. Mom didn't complain.

Until the medication kicked in, her confusion was off the charts. She was obsessed with her Word-Find puzzles and thought words could be found in the closet or drawers. She even thought she had words in her socks. Attempting to reason with her only caused her to become irritated and anxious. She was upset that I didn't believe her. To appease her, I would look in the closet and announce, "Nope, no words here." It's just easier than arguing.

Mom gets bored in her hospital room, and I'm pretty certain she's caused some disruption to the nursing staff because they placed a hospital chair with a tray in the hallway for her to sit on. She can watch the comings and goings and work on her Word-Finds. They consider her a fall risk, so the chair is equipped with an alarm if she should get up. I imagine she is still somewhat disruptive as she tried twice to get up while I was visiting. I explained the alarm on her chair and the reason for it, but she doesn't remember it very long.

October, week 4 (forty-three weeks)

Mom ended up having to do some recuperation in a nursing home. The bladder infection really took its toll on her. She is very unsteady and weak. Karen and I have taken turns visiting her so that one of us sees her every day.

Mom asked me yesterday if this was where she lived. It's a very small room with one faded picture on the wall and worn furnishings that appear to be at least fifty years old. She looked so pathetic sitting on the edge of her bed as she asked that question. I assured her that this was a temporary situation until she got a bit stronger. She had forgotten that she had been hospitalized. She will have some physical therapy, and I urged her to be as cooperative as possible so that she can gain strength and get back to her home.

I'm getting emotionally worn. I feel sympathy for Mom, yet I'm realizing that I also feel resentment. I fear that I begrudge Mom for getting old, for getting sick. I want my mother back! I want the mother who used to go shopping with me and treat me to lunch. I want the mother who went on trips with me. I want the mother who listened when I vented.

I have to keep reminding myself that her illness is not her fault. I looked up some devotions on resentment, learning that it leads to bitterness. I don't want to wallow in that negativity. I want joy and peace. I will be amending my prayer for patience to include a plea for protection from feelings of resentment.

November, week 1 (forty-four weeks)

Mom was released from the rehab facility. I don't think she liked the food there because she ate very little. I expect her appetite will return now that she's back home.

Though Mom has a refrigerator and microwave in her apartment, she no longer prepares any food there. She was a little surprised to learn they keep track of the meals she eats in the dining room and is billed for the two additional meals per day. After she thought about it a moment, she said that it's worth it because she can socialize. That's funny because after three months, she still doesn't know the names of those at her table. Maybe they don't know her name either.

Jamestown Estate has lots of activities that Mom participates in, which is good. She says she goes down to the lobby when there aren't activities and converses with other residents. That struck me as strange because I haven't yet witnessed anyone actually talking. When I visit and find Mom in the lobby, she is usually engrossed in her Word-Find book (one finger on the answer page because her ten-second patience level interferes with finding the word legitimately). Other residents are either napping or staring straight ahead at the wall (except for Ralph, who is watching the door). So if they are "conversing," it must be telepathically. I doubt they are aware of this gift they have. Just imagine if they harnessed this power! Ralph could influence people to open the door for him; they could convince the waitstaff to open the dining hall at four o'clock rather than four thirty. I will continue to observe this phenomenon; it requires further investigation.

November, week 2 (forty-five weeks)

For the past eight years, Sunday evening has been reserved, with very few exceptions, for dinner and Mexican Train Dominos with my mother at my house. I've told her to count on it unless I call, yet every Sunday, she calls to ask if we're getting together. That's 416 phone calls to date.

I'm rather amazed with her current situation that she can still play Dominos. She has trouble remembering what day it is, but she can play a mean game of Mexican Train, even counting and adding her tiles without assistance. This is serious business to her, and she frowns upon conversation while playing. Add to this the fact that she cheats! After a round, all the tiles are turned over and mixed up before each player selects fifteen tiles for the next round. She will turn over the tiles from her train and place her hand over that group, moving it around in a circle, never allowing those tiles to get into the mix with the others. Of course, those are the tiles she'll select; after all, they were connected into a train, so it's to her advantage. She thinks we don't notice. Sometimes this practice really bugs Allen, and during the mixing of the tiles stage, he will shove tiles at her to try and dislodge the group under her hand. This usually erupts into a mini battle of the two of them shoving tiles at each other. Aw, there's much to be said about a relaxing family game night.

November, week 3 (forty-six weeks)

We brought Mom over to my youngest son's new house for her to see it. We picked up takeout from a favorite Chinese restaurant of ours on the way over.

Pierce and Missy gave us the tour, and then we sat down to enjoy the chow mein. Missy set a couple of packets of soy sauce by each person's plate as we began to pass the containers. Mom picked up the packet and asked what it was. I had already grown impatient with her for a number of reasons that day, and my response to her question was "What do you think it is?" I asked that in somewhat of a sarcastic tone. She answered her usual, "I don't know." I just find it impossible to believe that she cannot remember common items that she has used or seen in everyday life for years. I want her to think before she asks a question.

I met Debra for dinner this week and shared this story of my annoyance with Mom. She didn't have sympathy for my plight. She said, "You're mean. Why didn't you just tell her what it was?"

I don't know.

It's a good question. Why did it irritate me? Why couldn't I simply answer and leave it at that? Why don't I believe that she really doesn't recognize things?

I don't want to be mean.

November, week 4
(forty-seven weeks)

My mother has always enjoyed keeping records. She would write down the time we left on a road trip, the miles we drove, and the time we arrived. She would write down every cent she spent on any given trip. When packing up her apartment to move into the assisted-living facility, I came across several small notebooks with such records. She never referred back to these notes once documented; they really had no point or purpose. Though, if she'd have ever found herself in the position of being in a courtroom with a lawyer asking, "Where were you on the night of . . . ?" she would be able to answer with details of how long she was there, how many miles away it was, and exactly what she spent before, during, and after being there. How many of us could do that? All these logs found their way to the trash; no way was I going to pack and move them.

Now she is keeping new records; she's taking attendance. She asks what day it is and glances at one of her many clocks (she has a strange attraction to clocks—there are three in her living room alone). Then she jots down your name, date, and time of your visit in the back of her Word-Find puzzle book. I guess if I was ever entertaining the idea to take advantage of her poor memory and considered fibbing about the frequency of my visits, I'd best rethink that.

Yes, memory loss and confusion are sad things, but if I can find a bit of humor in the situation, I can deal with it better. Given a choice of response between annoyed or amused, I'll choose amused.

December, week 1
(forty-eight weeks)

Apparently, impatience is a given when you are elderly. Mom's wait limit is down to fifteen seconds. At Jamestown Estate, she was given a call button on a cord that she's supposed to wear around her neck and can use in an emergency—for instance, if she fell or if she got disoriented and lost. She's also on a program for them to administer her meds. They come morning, noon, and night at around eight. I discovered she's using her call button to get those nurses off their butts to come at 8:01. She's allowed two calls per month and charged for anything additional. Mom manages to find new and interesting ways to spend her money!

I brought her home at exactly 8:07 last night after our Sunday dinner and a game or two of dominos. The place was a ghost town. There was not a moving creature on either the first or second floors. I assume they were all in their rooms getting ready for bed. I am now adding panic to the list of geriatric attributes. Mom was concerned they had already been by her apartment with her meds. I tried to assure her they'd be back. Finally, I succumbed to her expressions of concern and began to wander the halls looking for a nursing assistant (I wouldn't let Mom use her call button). Lesson learned: get Mom back by 7:59 PM.

December, week 2
(forty-nine weeks)

Mom wanted to show me her mail because there were items that confused her. We headed to the elevator, went up to the second floor, walked the fairly long hallway to her apartment, and then I asked her where her cane was. She'd mislaid it *again*. I take this common occurrence as proof positive that she doesn't *need* the cane. We walked back and found it near a chair in the rotunda. Then she was happy.

We went back to her apartment to go through her mail. The items she was anxious about were basically junk mail. It seems she thinks she must respond to each piece of mail. I explained they were just advertisements, but she still acted concerned, so I put them in my purse and told her I'd take of them. She was satisfied with that.

She is very happy in her new place and takes every opportunity to express that feeling. Even though Ralph annoys her by following her everywhere, the plus side to her memory loss is that she forgets about Ralph in a matter of minutes. When I told her that Ralph directed me where to find her one day, she asked, "Who's Ralph?" I told her he was the fellow in the wheelchair that follows her. She asked me to describe him. So either the four other fellows in wheelchairs are all following her too or she has forgotten about how irritated she gets when Ralph is in hot pursuit. She sure does live in the moment.

I found out that Ralph has a wife named Ruby who visits him daily. Apparently, she looks quite a bit like Mom. One morning, Ralph stopped me by the elevator and asked me to tell Ruby (he meant Mom) that she should come home. He said she won't listen to him. I'm thankful for that. If Mom was confused enough and went with Ralph to his apartment, that could cause some commotion when Ruby showed up!

For some reason, I keep playing that Kenny Rogers song in my head—"Ruby, don't take your love to town."

December, week 3 (fifty weeks)

Christmas is this week. The plan is to pick up Mom and bring her over to my house on Christmas Eve for the festivities. We'll enjoy dinner with the entire family and open gifts after dessert.

The last couple of years, Mom decided giving money to everyone was what she wanted to do rather than shop for gifts. She would pick up Christmas cards from the dollar store, write a name on the envelope, and stuff a bill inside each card. This year, she produced a box of blank envelopes and asked for my assistance. She couldn't remember the names of the great-grandchildren. I showed her the list we had written up months ago and placed in her calendar.

I took her to the bank to get enough ten-dollar bills to fill all the envelopes. She wanted to take out more money because she was below her comfort level in her wallet. I tried explaining she didn't need to carry a lot of cash around, but she wasn't listening. I also suggested she could leave money at the reception desk at her building for withdrawal prior to taking the van to a store, but she was not on board with that idea either. She doesn't trust them.

It's so difficult to try and reason with Mom. I find myself losing patience and employing a tone of voice that is less than kind or respectful. There are some areas that are too important to back down on; I just don't know how to win the argument.

December, week 4 (fifty-one weeks)

Karen and I generally visit Mom on different days and then touch base with each other. Karen asked about the cash Mom usually carries, commenting that it was forty dollars less than when she checked it last week. Mom can't remember spending anything. The facility van takes residents to the store or the bank, and Mom may have gone shopping, but she has always been very thrifty, and we can't imagine what she spent forty dollars on. We looked for receipts, since she doesn't throw anything away, but couldn't find any. We decided we're going to pay closer attention to her wallet.

Mom still insists on carrying a purse. I picked her up an inexpensive purse that sports a faux leather bow and is embellished with a few shiny beads. She likes bling. I packed it with tissues, pencils, a Word-Find book, and an old wallet that only has her library card and an expired AARP card in it. Her real wallet is kept in another purse, tucked on a shelf in her closet. We don't think it's a good idea for her to carry around money and all her identification. She's satisfied with the purse I styled for her.

I mentioned to Karen that I wanted to go through Mom's jewelry and bring home anything of value for safekeeping. Karen agreed that would be a good idea. Mom doesn't like when we go through her things, so I will have to do this when Karen can keep her busy. She won't understand our concern regarding her valuables.

December, week 5
(fifty-two weeks, one year)

To the left of the reception desk at Jamestown Estate is a wall of post office boxes numbered for each apartment. Mom stood behind a fellow who was simply emptying his mail slot. The problem was that her mailbox is below his slot; therefore, he was blocking her access. She very rudely suggested he move out of her way. I tried to nicely correct her and suggested she try being patient. I felt sorry for the guy; Mom's tone and her furrowed brow to accompany the harsh directive would make anyone recoil. I felt embarrassed. I had to remind myself that I'm not responsible for her behavior. It's just so strange to witness. She was the one who taught me to be kind and considerate.

Since one of the pieces of mail was her bank statement, I suggested we balance her checkbook. While going through her checkbook, I was looking at her and thinking there was something not quite right. I finally realized she had forgotten to draw in her eyebrows. Then I remembered Grandma, who seemed happy if the choppy, staggered lines were anywhere on her forehead. I decided that choosing between no eyebrows at all or a Picasso on your face, well, I'd choose the former.

I took the opportunity to employ creative lying and suggested that the balancing of the checkbook was too extensive and I would need to finish it at my home. I promised I would bring it back once I finished. That was the lying part. Both Karen and I feel that I need to take over her accounts.

I am hoping Mom will forget about the checkbook. I was able to put the statement and checkbook in my purse with her suspect approval.

Soon, it will be a year since Mom's doctor contacted me to express his concerns. A year ago, I was defending her, enjoying my ignorance of her condition. I now acknowledge she is ill and her brain is shrinking. I see the progression of the disease. A year ago, she was living on her own, driving a car, and maintaining her affairs. Now her independence is virtually gone. I never imagined this scenario.

January, week 1 (fifty-three weeks)

Mom was admitted to the Intensive Care Unit at the hospital after a fall. She has two fractured ribs and a displaced one (whatever that means). Besides the bruised and broken ribs, she is suffering dehydration.

She doesn't remember the fall. It's frustrating not to know how it happened. Apparently, she was found in the doorway of her unit. No one seems to know any details. No one knows how long she lay on the floor before she was noticed.

She wasn't wearing her call button. I've found it several times on her dresser and made her put it on, explaining its purpose. She doesn't understand. Even if she wore it, I doubt she would remember to press the button.

She looks so feeble in the hospital bed. This is a look I don't recall ever seeing before. Mom may have been timid and insecure in her early days, but the mother I knew most of my life was confident and in control. Venturing out into the workforce caused her to find that confidence, but it also caused stress on her marriage, which ended shortly after. She learned independence from that trial in her life. She turned the negatives into episodes of learning, becoming stronger and more self-assured. I recall a time when I needed reassurance, and her words of wisdom to me were "If you learned something from an experience, then it wasn't wasted." She suffered many challenges and disappointments in life but always maintained a positive attitude. This poised, self-assured woman was the mother I admired. This helpless, confused woman is a stranger to me.

January, week 2 (fifty-four weeks)

Mom is still in the hospital. They are telling us that there are no beds available at any north side rehab centers. I'm confused that they want to release her because she still has issues; her hemoglobin is low along with her sodium level, and her white blood cell count is elevated. She runs a low-grade fever almost daily. I would be more comfortable with her in the hospital. I guess I'm thankful the rehab centers are all at capacity.

Apparently, low sodium is another contributor to confusion. She is about as Looney Tunes as can be! She has worked the Word-Find puzzles into every aspect of her day. She told me the bruise on her thigh was caused by words. She now spells how she feels; she was W-A-R-M yesterday.

January, week 3 (fifty-five weeks)

Mom was moved to the rehab center last week. Her confusion is not as extreme as it was, but she is not very happy; she doesn't smile and isn't interested in her puzzles. Yesterday, I walked her down to the lunchroom and found a game to play. It was Connect Five, and she appeared to grasp the concept, though I couldn't say that she enjoyed playing. I think she participated to appease me.

Visits are rough because there isn't conversation. Before, on occasion, she might ask what Allen was doing. Currently, she doesn't seem to care. I just tell her everything that's going on with everyone, including the cats. She listens and nods and sometimes comments, "Oh, really?"

The rehab center provided her with a walker, and it appears she may need it on a permanent basis. That should make her happy; it will put her closer to the dining room at the assisted-living facility.

Today, we successfully moved Mom back to her apartment. Of course, it was during the peak of a mini snowstorm this morning. The aide who was helping us check out asked Mom if she had a hat. Mind you, in my lifetime, I do not recall Mom ever wearing a hat, but this question created an extreme reaction. "Where's my hat? I need my hat! Where's my hat?" Finally, the aide took Mom's scarf and tied it around her head, which satisfied her. I don't know why we didn't think of that; we were too busy trying to convince her she didn't have a hat.

When we pulled up to her residence, Mom claimed not to recognize the building; but once inside, she knew exactly which chair was hers in the dining room. She also learned there was bingo scheduled for three o'clock, so she was excited for that. It's good to be home.

January, week 4 (fifty-six weeks)

My mother's mob name should be Louie Bananas. I knew she was feeling better in the rehab center when bananas began to appear on her nightstand. Ahh, she's back to stealing food. This goes way back to when we used to annually travel to Las Vegas. We loved our buffets! Karen and I followed the rules of no food leaving the buffet, but Mom was the rebellious one, and each night, food would show up on the hotel room dresser (we never saw her take any food, but it would mysteriously appear). It always began with a banana, and then possibly a cookie, a muffin, a bagel, and so on. These items never got eaten; by the last day of the trip, as we were packing, Mom would shove them all off the end of the dresser into the trash can. It must have been the exhilaration of the act of thievery that enticed her; the motivation didn't prove to be remotely about hunger.

After moving into the assisted-living facility, bananas began appearing on her kitchen counter. As it would turn black, Karen or I would throw it away; a fresh banana would take its place almost immediately. So after a week in the hospital and a week in the rehab center, when bananas began to appear again, I knew we were on the road to recovery.

February, week 1 (fifty-seven weeks)

Karen and I visited Mom at the same time one day. While Karen kept Mom busy, I went through her jewelry box looking for any pieces of value. There was a gold ingot necklace with small diamonds that I was searching for in particular. It was a gift from the bank when Mom retired, and I'm certain is quite valuable. Just as I came across the necklace, Mom came into the bedroom and asked what I was doing. I mentioned that she didn't wear this necklace any longer. She took it from me and put it over her head, stating that she could still wear it. I didn't want to instill the fear that people may steal from her, so I didn't explain my plan to remove valuable jewelry from the premises. She handed me back the necklace, and I hung it again in the jewelry box. I plan to make another attempt at pinching it a later time.

This is such a new feeling for us, the sense to protect Mom.

February, week 2 (fifty-eight weeks)

We're back to staggering our visits with Mom. She appears to be well healed and much happier than she was a couple of weeks ago. She has adjusted well to using a walker; it's as though she's always used one. She has become very possessive in regard to her walker, constantly afraid someone may lay claim to it. I looped a string of cheap beads on the crossbar to identify it as hers. She was very pleased with that solution.

Mom has begun to verbalize concern that she doesn't remember which apartment is hers. Karen wrote the apartment number on a piece of paper and taped it to the walker. Now when she says she doesn't know where her apartment is, we point at the note and she says, "Oh, that's right. I live in 208."

Not only is her memory going but also her confidence and creativity. Mom gained her confidence when she went to work at nearly forty years old. She was born with creativity. These attributes defined her. Daily, there is less of her.

February, week 3 (fifty-nine weeks)

When I visited Mom today, I found her in the lobby area near the lunchroom. She offered me coffee, which is available to residents and guests, so we sat at the little bistro table near the ice cream parlor sipping our coffee. Then she opened up a napkin and offered me a cookie. They appeared to be a variety of Christmas cookies (red and green sprinkles gave them away). I selected the Russian tea cake. As I consumed the cookie, I did the math. It was a Christmas cookie, and Christmas Eve was exactly two months ago. Considering this cookie was probably not baked on Christmas Eve, which makes it over two months old. Are Russian tea cakes supposed to have a chewy center? I asked her where she got the cookies. She couldn't remember.

Lesson learned, now shared: do not accept cookies from people with dementia.

February, week 4 (sixty weeks)

I finally found the opportunity to rummage through Mom's jewelry. I was sick to my stomach when I realized the gold ingot necklace was missing. I wished I had used creative lying that day she caught me attempting to take it and manufactured some story of how I was going to have it cleaned or something. I don't know for sure what happened to it; Mom may have given it away. In that case, shame on the person who accepted it. I just have to keep telling myself that it was a thing, just a thing.

Over the last couple of months, Mom has gone through close to $300 that we can't account for. We had decided to inventory her wallet at each visit and discovered twenty to forty dollars would be missing each time. Karen took the last ten dollars out of Mom's wallet and left a note that stated, "It's all gone!"

I absolutely hate that we are considering that staff may be stealing from Mom. We can't imagine how else the money is going missing unless Mom is giving it away. This disturbs us greatly. Mom, however, doesn't even realize her money is missing. She only knows when it's below the amount that she has determined she must carry. We are now refusing to allow her to keep money on her. She hasn't made a trip to the bank in a while. Maybe that's another area that's creating confusion for her.

Mom has stated a couple of times that she thinks something is wrong with her head. We don't know how to respond to that. Somehow, I think actually telling her that she has dementia is not the right thing to do. We just tell her that everyone forgets once in a while.

March, week 1 (sixty-one weeks)

I think my mother believes my phone is hardwired to my brain. This has happened several times now when she feels she must reach me (and pretty much everything is urgent with her these days). She will leave an initial message; it always begins with "This is your Mother," not "This is Mom"; no, it's "Mother," rather like "the Admiral." The next message she leaves (about five minutes later) is more intense. After another five minutes, the tone has become irritated and demanding. "Would you *please* call me back!" If it gets to a fourth or fifth message, it's "Why won't you pick up your phone?" like I'm purposely ignoring her. In less than a half hour, she can accelerate from slightly needy to a stalking terrorist.

When I call her back, she has either forgotten why she called in the first place or the reason for needing to reach me was minor, definitely not the emergency status she made it out to be.

Mom has become demanding and more impatient. That adds to my aggravation level. I fear I will never achieve patience when dealing with her.

March, week 2 (sixty-two weeks)

I met Debra for dinner this week. I was in a foul mood, complaining about how busy and stressed I was, and how Mom was relentless in finding new ways to irritate me. Midway through our bacon cheeseburgers, Debra commented, "It's not all about you, Maggie."

I could have taken offense, but she was right. She is a true friend who will not agree with me for the sake of agreeing; she will say what I need to hear.

Toward the end of the cheeseburger, we were talking about how dementia works, and Debra was urging me to realize and accept that Mom truly does not remember having ever eaten a potato or using a packet of soy sauce. It is not an act; it's fact. She talked about her mother and her reactions to things she has said or done. Debra is sympathetic to my situation but not to my attitude. Pretty much her advice was "Don't allow these things to annoy you." It's my choice how I react. I need to have empathy for Mom, because it's not all about me.

March, week 3 (sixty-three weeks)

My sister and I have concluded that Mom's brain has become that of a set of index cards with appropriate statements and responses. In most any circumstance, she flips through the cards and selects the one she feels fits. The ones that get the most use are "Oh, really?" "Oh, that's terrible," and "I can't remember." There are times when the cards seem to have been dropped and they've gotten shuffled out of order; her response will be tragically off topic. For instance, I would relate a cute story, and she'll pull the "Oh, that's terrible" card.

Then there's the wild card that has "ha ha ha ha ha" on it because she finds amusement constantly, appropriate or not.

She recently added a new card. Let me clarify that my mother has *never* been one to swear. Growing up, we couldn't even say "pee" or "fart." Her new card that she pulls out whenever frustrated (which is quite often, considering her impatience) is one word—"shit." She can't get the seat belt fastened—pull out the new card. Doesn't have the number called in bingo—pull out the new card. I guess it could be worse. I just hope she'll remain satisfied with that one swear word and not discover another harsher one!

March, week 4 (sixty-four weeks)

I was in Mom's apartment waiting for the time to go down for lunch, and two aides showed up to administer her noon medications. Maybe it's my imagination, but they appeared surprised to see me and acted in an awkward fashion, as though they'd been caught at something. There is no reason two aides are needed for this task unless one is in training, and that's the assumption I made.

After Mom took her pills, she asked them, "What do I owe you?" There was a moment of silence, and then I told Mom that it was their job to give her pills and she didn't have to pay them. Neither one of the aides made any comment; they just left. It made me wonder if that is where Mom's cash went. It would be an easy score because the victim wouldn't complain, since they don't even remember.

I do not like this feeling of distrust that I'm experiencing.

March, week 5 (sixty-five weeks)

Mom had another hospital stay for low sodium. She was in the hospital for four days. They aren't sure why she's having issues with retaining sodium but have prescribed a medication to hopefully correct the problem.

Mom noticed her wristband had "DNR" boldly printed on it. She asked what it meant. It was obviously for "do not resuscitate," but I didn't think she would understand at this point. Creative lying is coming much easier to me these days; I said, "Department of Natural Resources." Fortunately, she didn't ask for further explanation.

When they suggested a few days of rehab, Karen voiced her apprehension and stood firm. She expressed our observation and concern that the rehab stays actually exacerbated the hospital stay setbacks for Mom. We felt she would do better if allowed to go home from the hospital to a familiar place. I was surprised that they succumbed and released Mom to return to her apartment.

When we got Mom home, Ralph was so happy to see her. He wheeled up with a huge smile and tugged at her sleeve. She barely gave him an acknowledgement nod; poor love-struck Ralph.

April, week 1 (sixty-six weeks)

I joined Mom for lunch today. They serve really good food, and it only costs me five dollars. Sometimes they run out of a featured selection, so now I understand the rush to get in and get seated; a full table gets to order first.

Mom doesn't converse much, so I try to engage the entire table. Marie is the most fun to chat with because she will actually converse and make sense. She does repeat herself somewhat, but I don't mind. She's very proud of her daughters and has told me several times that one of them is a teacher.

I don't believe Esther had her hearing aids in today because I was describing a house plant I just bought, and she kept saying, "Cantaloupe? Cantaloupe?" I didn't know how to respond.

Jane's seat was empty. Priscilla was consuming any food items that the others didn't care to eat. Mom was focused on her plate of food. She tends to hover over her plate appearing as though she's done time in "the Big House." She won't converse at all when she can use her mouth for eating; hence, I never have to say, "Don't talk with your mouth full."

It was a nice lunch. Then Marie spit food on me; she didn't mean to but was talking with her mouth full. I planned to ignore the bit of potato on the back of my hand until I could wipe it off unobserved, but Marie pointed it out. I could only chuckle and say, "It happens to all of us."

April, week 2 (sixty-seven weeks)

I think my mother is taking the assigned seating for meals a bit too seriously. Last weekend, we had family gathered at our house for a birthday celebration. My dining room table was set, and I noticed her checking it out. Mom usually sits next to me at the table, and my seat is the closest to the kitchen for me to pop up and down as needs arise. Pretty soon, she brought her purse over and put it on her chair. Apparently, she must have felt that wasn't obvious enough, so she placed a used tissue on her plate. Now that would pretty much deter anybody from wanting to sit there! I didn't much appreciate that addition to my lovely table, but we're all family, and family understands.

Before I called everyone to sit up, I was exchanging a few words with Mom as I scampered between the kitchen and dining room with serving dishes. Mom, by now, had positioned her body behind her chair. Evidently, my sister-in-law came too close to Mom's claimed seat, and Mom announced fairly loudly that this was her place to sit. Patty just smiled and assured her she wasn't going to take her spot. I love family; they can be so gracious!

April, week 3 (sixty-eight weeks)

Mom has become fixated on time. The other Sunday, when I picked her up to take her out to dinner, she mused, "I can't believe it's quarter to five. Where did the day go?" I attempted to update her on the grandkids, and her response was "It's five to five. The day's almost over." I tried to get her to pick a restaurant, but she told me that she doesn't get out to eat much (only every Saturday with my sister). Then she added, "It's five o'clock. It feels like morning." I was granted a fifteen-minute break before the next time announcement.

Later, it dawned on me that asking Mom where she wanted to dine was asking her an impossible to answer question. I don't think she can remember places like restaurants. She continues to do some degree of masking, and rather than admit she can't recall things, she will conjure an excuse. I tend to get annoyed when she won't answer questions. I have to consider she may legitimately not know the answer, as simple as it seems to me.

I discovered that taking a deep breath when I begin to feel irritated really helps. Mom doesn't know she's being annoying. She's not doing it on purpose; she thinks she's making conversation when she's making her time announcements. Training myself to be understanding rather than reactive is hard work.

April, week 4 (sixty-nine weeks)

I noticed Jane wasn't at the table a couple of times and made the mistake of pointing that out when I joined them for lunch today. Others at the table informed me they don't ask because, since you're not family, you're told nothing. They simply accept it when someone disappears. I felt like I was in a Stephen King story! People just go missing and no one knows why. They didn't seem disturbed by it, which made it feel all the more spooky.

The cloud was lifted when the staff brought in a helium-filled balloon for Delores at table three. They announced it was her birthday and asked everyone to join in singing Happy Birthday. It was pretty amazing as people who appeared nearly catatonic a moment before began belting out the familiar song. It was loud and joyous. Then it was over, and people immediately reverted to their previous state. It was a strange lunch hour.

May, week 1 (seventy weeks)

On a visit when both of us went at the same time, Karen noticed Mom had folded paper towels on the bathroom counter next to an empty toilet paper roll and asked Mom about it. Mom claimed to have run out of toilet tissue. I checked the closet and found a dozen rolls. I guess that's the problem—they were all in the closet; out of sight, out of mind.

I hope flushing paper towels will not create a plumbing problem. We've decided not to mention this to the staff; we'll just wait and see.

Mom complained again that she really wished she had her car. She would have gone to the store to buy toilet paper if she had her car. We reminded her about the van she could take to the store, or better yet, she could call one of us to take her to the store. Realizing these statements weren't being accepted well, we changed the subject. Her issue wasn't the toilet paper or the store; it was her car that she no longer had and the loss of her independence.

May, week 2 (seventy-one weeks)

It's always an experience joining Mom for lunch. Before Mom even sat down, she complained that everyone else gets served, but she never does. I reminded her she hadn't ordered yet; in fact, she hadn't even looked at the menu. The entire lunchtime was one complaint after the other, not only from Mom but also from everyone at the table. They all appeared to be in a mood. It was very tense.

Nancy, a new addition to their table, was irritated that they had cut her sandwich in small pieces. Marie thought her pickle was too small. Esther was upset that she had consumed her juice, and the waitstaff hadn't noticed in the five seconds she allowed them.

The dessert was a cookie of which there was a variety to pick from. Esther wanted the brown one like Mom's. The waitress brought her a white one, explaining they were out of the other, in which Mom complained wasn't any good anyway. Esther mumbled, "I don't believe it. That girl just doesn't like me for some reason." Gee, do you suppose it's because you complain every waking second?

May, week 3 (seventy-two weeks)

Mom seems to be having more bad days when she doesn't comprehend that behind the closet door are many, many outfits to pick from. She doesn't recall what she wore the day before. At night, when she readies herself for bed, she hangs up the clothes she wore on a rack in the corner of her bedroom. In the morning, she apparently sees the clothes on the rack and puts them on. She wore the same outfit three days in a row last week. When I pointed that out to her, she responded in a belligerent tone that sometimes she wears an outfit four days in a row.

Years ago, Mom made me promise to tell her if she ever smelled bad. Grandma had begun to repeat clothing without laundering, and it resulted in a nose-numbing odor. Mom never wanted to get to that point. Well, she was there. I tried to tell her as kindly as I could that by not changing her clothes, she had begun to smell badly. Her response was irritated denial. I told her of the promise she had me make, but she didn't recall it. I guess keeping my promise on this topic was not a wise choice.

I suppose I shouldn't let her clothing bother me, but it does. At least I don't react to Mom with a raised voice or condescending tone any longer. Instead, I try to figure out a way to amend the issue.

I'll try hanging a different outfit on her rack in the bedroom and hope she selects the clean one.

May, week 4 (seventy-three weeks)

Today, I joined Mom for dinner. I got there at 4:27 and wouldn't you know they let them into the dining room five minutes early! They were already being served as I waited for a chair and a place to be set for me. There was no conversation happening at Mom's table, and I envied a couple of other tables that seemed to have a good volley of dialogue going.

By the time I was served, Mom was finishing her ice cream. Then she looked at her watch, and the announcements began. "It's ten to five. Where does the time go?" Ten minutes later, she remarked, "It's five in the morning already." Maybe I'm not supposed to correct her, but I did. That started the entire table debating whether it was morning. Perhaps that was the conversation I earlier envied from the other tables. Eventually, my mother was the only holdout for the morning argument, and she appeared to give in, though not happy about it. A short while later, she asked me if I was coming back tonight. I told her it *was* night. Hopefully, as it gets dark, she'll figure it out.

June, week 1 (seventy-four weeks)

The facility has recommended that we consider memory care for Mom. There is a secure area of the third floor dedicated to memory care for the more-advanced dementia sufferers. The director and the head nurse feel Mom should be moved there. Of course, we asked why; we thought she was fitting in and functioning well. They cite her confusion. Our argument is that the bladder infection and low-sodium issues created the confusion. They told us that Mom asks several times a day when lunch or dinner is served. We know it's irritating to answer the same question over and over again, but sometimes we think Mom just wants to converse and can't think of anything to say, so she asks a question. It just happens to be the same question all the time.

Mom needs some attention at times, but this is an assisted-living facility. Assist!

June, week 2 (seventy-five weeks)

I'm wondering if there's a connection between dementia and hoarding. I took a monthlong stack of *Today's Events* from her desk to put on the recycle pile. I mean, really, do we need to know exactly what went on at one thirty last Wednesday? Well, I was stopped dead! Oh, no—she planned to take care of that, don't touch! I'm certain they will be there (only a thicker pile) next visit. Maybe Mom is feeling that she has no control over anything in her life any longer. If she can control the stack of paper on her desk, at least that's something, and she's going to fight to maintain the control.

Another argument for hoarding is the candy that is appearing at an alarming rate in her apartment. Apparently, you win tiny pieces of candy when you play the games that are played there. She's up to three bowls overflowing in various locations in her apartment. I don't think she ever eats a piece—they are trophies. I don't think I'm allowed to eat a piece—they are trophies.

June, week 3 (seventy-six weeks)

Often, Jamestown Estate provides entertainment for the residents. Today, I arrived during the middle of a performance of a man who sang, accompanied by a pianist. They were both quite talented, and the residents were engrossed. Mom had a spot in the front row, on the end, so she could keep her hand on her walker.

I watched from a distance, hoping Mom wouldn't notice me. I know if she saw me, she would leave the entertainment to join me. I wanted her to continue to enjoy the program. When it was over, I approached Mom, and she was thrilled to see me. I allowed her to treat me to an ice cream from the parlor.

It's been a couple of months since I've had her over for dinner and dominoes. I've discovered that she seems more anxious being away from her residence. Outings aren't enjoyable for her any longer. She's much happier when I visit, and she can treat me to an ice cream.

Instead of weekly outings, I will plan on having her join us for special events and holidays. Hopefully, she'll be fine with that. I don't know that she recalls that we've had her over every Sunday for nearly eight years; she never mentions it.

June, week 4 (seventy-seven weeks)

There wasn't a scheduled activity in the afternoon when I arrived to visit Mom today. I remembered she had a game of Yatzee in her drawer and decided to give that a try with her. She actually did pretty well but usually asked me which dice she should keep, and I'd have to show her which space to fill in the score. It was almost like playing yourself in a game of Yatzee. Regardless, it kept her occupied, and she seemed to enjoy my company. She was able to add the dice and add her score. I find that amazing.

We played two games, which took about forty-five minutes. I still find that short visits are the best for her and for me. I told her I was heading home to make dinner for Allen, an excuse that she was fine with. As I leave the building, she stands and waves until I'm out of sight.

June, week 5 (seventy-eight weeks)

They brought up Mom's memory problems again and restated the recommendation for her to be moved to the memory care unit. The bedrooms in this section are all shared; they call them "companion rooms." I really have trouble imagining Mom being happy with someone else sharing her space. Then there's the issue of the bathroom; there's no way she will tolerate another person using her bathroom. She keeps all her lipsticks, hair clips, and toiletries neatly displayed on the countertop in *her* bathroom.

We decided we will, at the very least, tour the memory care area. We'll set up an appointment after the holiday weekend. I still don't understand what qualifies Mom for this move. The director is busy selling us on this idea, claiming that they can offer Mom so much more in this environment versus the assisted-living program. I remain skeptical.

Again, I'm feeling like I have no life beyond the needs of my mother. I don't want to resent her, but I battle that feeling. I understand the disease is progressive, but I feel it's progressing faster than I can come to grips with it. I may need to arrange another dinner with Debra for a pep talk.

July, week 1 (seventy-nine weeks)

I picked Mom up on Fourth of July for a cookout. She wasn't waiting for me as usual, so I had to search her out. I found her with about ten others playing a game of card bingo. The game was quite intense; not one person acknowledged my presence. I stood next to Mom for a good five to ten minutes, and she didn't even notice. They play this game for money, so they are very focused. By watching a couple of rounds, I understood that you're dealt a certain number of cards, and then another deck is used to call a card, which you discard if you have it, with the goal of getting rid of all your cards. There was slight chaos when aces were called as most of the residents threw in their eights; then the others (those with better hearing) would loudly correct them. The game finally ended when Priscilla yelled, "Bingo!" She was awarded the pot, a take of about fifty cents, enough for an ice cream at the parlor. I felt guilty taking Mom away from the game—the next round was for a dime, which could be a one-dollar pot (an ice cream for her and for me).

July, week 2 (eighty weeks)

Karen and I gained admittance to the memory care section along with the director of sales for Jamestown Estate. She was very enthusiastic to show us this area. We entered through the door with the security code lock and were surprised to be stepping into a room crammed with residents in chairs with their walkers in front of them and several wheelchairs, each occupied by a frail-looking person. They were all placed in front of a television, but no one appeared to be engaged in what was being broadcast. They resembled puppies in a pound; all looking at us with a hopeful "pick me" expression.

We walked through the entry room, which led to the dining area that doubled as the activity center. They were cleaning up after lunch, and it appeared they fed a lot of very messy people. The dining area was small and lacked the stylish décor of the assisted-living dining room. The walls of the memory care section were devoid of decoration, unlike the rest of the facility. It looked institutional. We then walked down the drab hallway and peered into rooms, which all had two beds and one bathroom.

The director was jabbering about how proud they were of the new programs they were instigating in this section, but we weren't listening. We were busy fighting off tears. We didn't have to speak to express our disappointment. We recognized the signs in each other; the skinny lips, the shiny eyes blinking back tears, the crumpled brow. It felt like people were placed here to be forgotten.

We decided as soon as we left the building that we would be checking out a new place for Mom to live. This place is firm that she no longer would be a resident in the assisted-living area. There must be other options out there.

July, week 3 (eighty-one weeks)

Karen and I have been checking out other assisted-living/memory care places for Mom. We were happy to find that there are places that don't appear like a 1950s hospital. Granted, the memory care sections are different than assisted living, with residents on lockdown, and more aides about. Many of the residents appear to be low functioning, requiring much attention. It's somewhat sad but not awful.

Mom was tested by a nurse at one of the facilities; another Mini Mental with which she did not fare well. We were so certain that she didn't need memory care; it was difficult to come to terms with the reality of her stage of dementia. We couldn't argue with the results of the testing. We had been so busy defending Mom that we hadn't acknowledged the changes.

Obviously, there is an increase of cost for care. That's a minor concern at this point; Mom still has lots of money. We are somewhat concerned if she will notice the change in residents. Will she think we've committed her to a loony bin?

Of the memory care units we toured, we liked two places. The comparison in a nutshell: one gave us fresh baked banana walnut bread in a cellophane bag with a gold tie; the other gave us a Rice Krispie bar on a foam plate.

July, week 4 (eighty-two weeks)

We did it! We chose banana bread over Krispie bar. We had to admit the truth; the dementia is progressing, and Mom is ready for memory care.

Her apartment at Rosewood will be a studio style where the bedroom and living area are combined. The small kitchen has a mini refrigerator but no stove. There's a small entry where we plan to put a drop-leaf table and two chairs. She will have to give up her dining room set, curio, a dresser, and the love seat. It is a much smaller place than what she had, with much less closet space. We will need to rotate her wardrobe as the seasons change.

The common areas of this facility are richly decorated and furnished beautifully. There is a warm, comfortable feel to the building. There are several specialized areas for all residents to enjoy. One spot has a dressing table with a mirror and racks of hats, jewelry, and other accessories. Another area has realistic-looking dolls with a changing table and infant clothing. There's a tool bench for the men and a gardening area on the deck.

We just couldn't bring ourselves to put her in an institutional setting versus a luxury vacation location (with a price tag to go with it). Heck, it's her money, not ours! It may be a year until we have to consider something else with a lesser cost, but while she's still fairly aware and appreciative of the finer things—it's banana bread for our mother!

August, week 1 (eighty-three weeks)

This time, we didn't even tell Mom she was moving. It was quite the covert mission involving nearly all of our family members. My niece Jillian sat with Mom playing a game with other residents, while we scurried back and forth with boxes and carts no more than twenty feet away from them. Mom never noticed; she was engrossed in the game. It was Jillian's job to be sure she didn't venture back to her apartment.

We all ate lunch with Mom at the old place, and she asked several times who everyone was (ten of us; daughters, son-in-laws, grandchildren). She knows Karen and seems to know me but mixes me up with Jillian. The level of confusion she displayed convinced me that her dementia has progressed quite a bit this past year.

While the guys drove the U-Haul, we took Mom in the car. We waited until we pulled into the lot of Rosewood to tell her this was her new home. We explained we were concerned with the level of care she had been receiving and this place was better. The staff at Rosewood got her involved in an activity immediately upon arrival. That helped a lot as we worked to get furniture and boxes moved in and unpacked. It was a little awkward when she asked when she was going home. Of course, we told her this was home now.

Chester, the third-floor orange cat, made a visit to her apartment when she was getting into bed. He walked in like he owned the place, greeted her, sniffed around a bit, and left. Mom was happy that the cat left; she didn't want an animal in her place and made that fact known. Once Chester had vacated the premises, Mom appeared to settle in just fine.

Our plan is to visit daily for a while until we're convinced she's comfortable.

August, week 2 (eighty-four weeks)

It seems that Mom is acclimating to the new place. The inmates all seem crazy; then I realize my denial of my mother's condition and recognize she's where she belongs. She doesn't ask about the former place or any of the people. She appears not to notice some of the more-colorful residents in this place. Possibly she's forgotten what normal is.

We sat in the common area waiting for an activity to begin, and Mom pointed out the people asleep in chairs and laughed at them. Ten seconds later, she nodded off.

August, week 3 (eighty-five weeks)

After a year of Mom being in assisted living at Jamestown Estate, I was familiar with several of the residents (I'm missing Ralph terribly). I'm starting anew at this place.

The other day, a woman stopped by the table where Mom and I were working on a jigsaw puzzle. She made some statements in a conversational tone, but I couldn't make sense of what she was saying. Not to be rude, I waited until she left before asking Mom what she said. Mom had already forgotten she had even been there, so couldn't be of help.

Yesterday, I passed by this same woman; dressed nicely, makeup well applied, and hair impeccably styled. She smiled and stated, "They learned to color." I've decided not to attempt to make sense of her statements; I just nod and grin at her. Apparently, she lives in a state of nonsense and simply, literally says what comes to mind. I think I might add verbal response to my grin and nod, stuff like, "Ain't that the truth" or "Amen to that!" I must admit, I like her much better than the woman who randomly shouts, "Shut up!"

August, week 4 (eighty-six weeks)

I have noticed many differences in memory care versus assisted living. Mom doesn't seem to mind at all that she can't leave the third floor; in fact, it appears to comfort her. Another stress she doesn't have (three times a day) is ordering from a menu. A while back, my sister mentioned she thought Mom had forgotten how to read a menu. I'm realizing now that it wasn't the reading; it was the comprehending. Now I've gained the understanding that she no longer could read "hamburger" and visual it. We kept trying to make her decide what she wanted to eat, not realizing she couldn't. We'd be met with questions like, "Chips? Are they good? Do I like them?" Our reaction was annoyance and disbelief; how could she forget what a potato chip was? At Rosewood, they simply bring the choices out to the table, usually two or three, and the resident picks which one they want. How easy is that! For the last couple of years, she has been stressing out over what we would consider minor, commonplace things. It is so great for her to be in a facility that understands nothing is commonplace to someone with dementia.

August, week 5 (eighty-seven weeks)

There are residents on the third floor that are referred to as shoppers. That is a polite term for thief. They stroll about the floor checking for unlocked doors. If they should find one, they enter and begin their shopping experience. They take items that catch their eye, stuffing them in pockets or even under their shirt. If they should happen to find a container, it's an even better shopping experience. Hence, things go missing, but the staff generally knows where to find lost items.

Mom is good about locking her door; she occasionally forgets. One day, I suspect Mom had forgotten to lock her door because I found a small plastic storage box on her kitchen counter with several unrelated items in it. I assume someone entered to do some shopping, which must have been interrupted. I put the things away and reminded Mom of the importance of locking her door, but I suspect she won't remember.

September, week 1
(Eighty-eight weeks)

We celebrated Mom's eighty-eighth birthday by having Rosewood cater a Sunday lunch for our family on the first floor, which is assisted living. The residents on this floor are less likely to crash the party. The lunch was buffet style in a large common area that could accommodate our families, about fifteen of us.

I was impressed with how nicely the staff arranged the buffet of hamburgers, hotdogs, salads, and a few other items. Mom would have approved if she remembered how she used to enjoy entertaining. My folks often hosted their card club, and Mom would cook and create all day in preparation for the evening. She liked women's magazines and was unafraid to attempt dishes featured in these publications. She appreciated not only the quality of a dish for flavor but also the presentation. Her table was always a work of art. Karen and I looked forward to these gatherings because we would wear our best pajamas, greet the company, and be allowed to make a plate of food from Mom's buffet table and then hide away in the bedroom to enjoy these treats while we watched TV until we fell asleep. That was a fond memory that only Karen and I recall now.

We placed Mom in a comfy chair near the end of the buffet table, which may have been a mistake, since it was close to the plate of cookies. She must have eaten three before we began to serve ourselves lunch. Mom commented on *all the food* and kept asking who all the people were. It appears she only recognizes me, Karen, and Jillian. Mostly she sat and grinned at everyone. Often, she would ask how old she was and be shocked with the answer.

I was surprised that she didn't become anxious even after nearly an hour had passed. I think she understood that this gathering was in her honor, or unlimited cookies gave her solace.

September, week 2
(eighty-nine weeks)

Mom looked cute in her green pants with a purple, blue-and-green top, accessorized with green beads, earrings, and bracelet. We're paying the next level to have morning and evening assists with dressing. I thought whoever put her together today was very good at it and probably enjoyed the job. I complimented her on her all-together look. She replied that a man came to help her dress this morning.

I talked to my sister later, and she told me that Mom looked absolutely hideous in the morning when she visited. She had blue pants, a purple top, and red beads. Karen, though surprised, didn't say anything to Mom but suggested they go back to her room and look for different beads (she has at least fifty necklaces). Karen totally redressed her in the outfit I saw her in. Mom also told Karen about the man who dressed her. Karen asked at the desk before she left if they had a man on staff, and the answer was no. We're assuming the aide is someone flat-chested with short hair.

September, week 3 (ninety weeks)

"Bummer." The word for the day is "bummer." I visited Mom this afternoon, and she must have said "bummer" at least ten times (maybe twenty). Losing at bingo, "Bummer!" Understandable. But walking down the hall, "Bummer." Curious, I asked if something was wrong. Nope. Then I heard her voice from the bathroom, "Bummer." I didn't ask. Other than expressing this word, she had no physical complaints, seemed pleasant, comfortable, not crabby, and generally in good humor.

I did run across my friend who makes strange statements. Today, she had a disappointed look on her face as she said, "I thought mother would buy enough for all of us." Maybe Mom has also decided to respond to her. "Bummer" fits.

September, week 4
(ninety-one weeks)

Mom fell Monday night or Tuesday early morning. She's got a huge purple bump on her forehead. She doesn't remember falling. Karen spent half the day at the clinic on Tuesday to be sure she didn't fracture her skull. Mom is surprised every time she looks in the mirror, saying things like, "Oh my! What happened?" and "Where did that come from?" Between those moments of shock, she fills the time with asking what day and date it is, and checking the calendar. I think this is how she displays anxiety; she fixates on something like the date and will ask the same question every thirty seconds (literally). It majorly taxes one's patience. We haven't figured out a way to calm her—distraction doesn't seem to work.

October, week 1 (ninety-two weeks)

I like to work jigsaw puzzles with Mom when I visit. Conversation is something that has all but disappeared; working a puzzle with her feels like quality time, something we can do together. Often, I can tell if it's a good day or a bad day by how she approaches the puzzle. If she comprehends the concept of a puzzle, it's a good day. Today, she wanted to stack the pieces on top of each other and after a few moments scooped up all the pieces and put them in the box.

I really miss conversation with her. Sometimes I just talk about things we used to do. I'm learning not to say *remember*. I just start talking, eliminating the precursor to the topic, "Do you remember when . . ." Statements like that cause her to become uneasy, like she's expected to remember and can't. Once in a while, I will bring photos with me to show her to support the story I tell. She doesn't recall trips, family gatherings on holidays, or events. I do remember these things, and it makes me very sad that she doesn't share the memory any longer.

October, week 2
(ninety-three weeks)

Rosewood called yesterday to tell me Mom lost a tooth. I thought maybe she was acknowledging autumn with a new look, the jack-o'-lantern. It turns out she had removed and misplaced her "flapper" tooth apparatus (a removable cap). I think we'll just live with this.

When I visited today, Mom seemed fairly confused; she didn't remember she lived there and didn't know where her room was. Peggy, the lead aide, told me that Mom had wanted her to spend the night in her room because she doesn't like being alone at night.

A short time later, Mom asked me, as she pointed to Peggy, if I had met "him." That gave me something to ponder. She thinks Peggy is a guy, and she invited *him* to spend the night. I'm not sure if I'm ready to have this "talk" with Mom.

October, week 3 (ninety-four weeks)

At Jamestown Estate, we had to continue to use Mom's doctor and take her to appointments. At Rosewood, we signed up to use the doctor who is a geriatric specialist and makes house calls. That is such a nice feature. Also, with its nursing staff, this facility has the capability to gather fluids for performing lab testing, this way being able to discover an infection before it gets to the point of requiring hospitalization. They discovered Mom was suffering from a bladder infection, thus the confusion she had exhibited. They got her on antibiotics, and she seems to have improved over the last two days. I'm so happy that she didn't have to be hospitalized, since those stays create major setbacks for her.

I meant to try to teach Mom a new word to replace "bummer." I was thinking something like "awesome" or maybe "groovy." Too late; she already replaced it with, well, not exactly a word, more of an exclamation—"woo-hoo." I don't know where she picked it up, but it fills most all periods of silence that exceed ten seconds.

October, week 4 (ninety-five weeks)

Often, there are special events for all residents that occur in a large area on the second floor. They were bringing in a small petting zoo, and I thought Mom might enjoy that and possibly it would stimulate her memory, since her early years were spent on a farm.

It just so happened that at the same time, I was involved in the process of trying to gain access to her retirement accounts and needed to have Mom answer questions on the phone to prove her identity and grant me authorization to handle her affairs. I was trying to keep an eye on the group in the room, wanting to get her seated before the show began, and also attempting to run interference between Mom and the bank employee on the phone. Mom had trouble recognizing my cell phone as a telephone, which made it even more difficult. Pretty soon, I took the phone and repeated the questions to Mom. I explained to the woman on the phone that my mother had dementia and may not remember the answers to the questions. That didn't matter; the inquisition was going to happen. The questions all had multiple choice answers. I attempted to repeat the question with the three answers to Mom. By answer three, she had forgotten the question. Fortunately, I knew the answers and pretended to the person on the phone that Mom had responded. The questions were queries like, "Did you ever own a . . ." followed by three different makes and models of cars. "Did you ever live on . . ." followed by three different street names. There were at least six of these questions. Praise God, I got them all right. Then I was instructed to give Mom the phone again while they asked her if she would allow me access to her information. Mom answered yes, and this matter was resolved. Before disconnecting, I suggested I was not the only person in the situation of a parent with dementia, and possibly they should come up with another option in the future.

I left Mom in the room with the other residents, and the presentation began seconds after she was seated. I headed home, exhausted.

November, week 1
(ninety-six weeks)

Mom was really good today when I visited. I brought some photos of Christmases, birthdays, and trips. She enjoyed them even though she had to ask where each one was taken and who the people were. We looked through the pictures, she ate a Milky Way (I bring her a couple of packages of fun-size candy bars each week), worked on a jigsaw puzzle, and then it was time for bingo.

When I got her seated for the bingo game, I noticed she was wearing different glasses. I asked her about them and asked if she could see all right. She replied, "I suppose." So I asked the aide, and she said that Mom had two pairs. That was news to me. The aide went and got the other pair, which were much more ornate and were bifocals; I recognized this pair. I have no idea whose glasses she was wearing.

November, week 2
(ninety-seven weeks)

It's nice to see Mom in fresh, clean clothes each time I visit. She no longer smells. I don't mind paying for this level of care. This was one of the areas that I mentioned to the "dementia expert" shortly after she was diagnosed. He told me it wasn't important; it fell under let-her-have-her-way category. Maybe it isn't dangerous, but it isn't hygienic or pleasant for the nose. In this case, we found our way around letting her have her way. She doesn't complain about it, so everyone is happy.

Bathing assistance is also included in the level of care. We informed them that we believed she had developed an aversion to water and getting her into a tub may provide a challenge for them. We suspected she no longer bathed other than sponge baths, which she referred to as PTA (pits, twat, and ass). She didn't realize that "twat" was a bad word. When I informed her, she changed it to "tits." We noticed this on a five-day trip to Vegas a few years back; she never took a shower or ran a bath the entire trip. It was about the same time that she became less concerned with privacy, hers or ours. I was brushing my teeth in the motel bathroom, and she entered, ran warm water, soaped up a washcloth, and began vigorously washing between her legs. I was shocked and shut my eyes while brushing. After she felt she had accomplished her task in a satisfactory manner, she took the cloth and gingerly wiped up the counter. I shrieked, "Mom! My toothbrush was on that counter!"

November, week 3
(ninety-eight weeks)

They were just finishing dessert when I visited Mom today. Mom was disturbed because someone had left quite a mess of chocolate cake under their chair. She pointed it out to me and then to the aide and then to me again. Finally, I decided to get her away from the mess. We went for a walk around the hall.

She wasn't sure where her apartment was, but as we turned the corner, she said we had to walk all the way to the end of the hall; that was good recall.

Outside her door is a photo box I put together with pictures of the three of us. We looked at it awhile, and she commented about the old pictures when she had dark hair. Her favorite is a photo of Karen, her, and me from a Christmas Eve gathering a few years ago. She said, "I like this one the most." I remarked, "Look, that's when you were taller than either of us!" She laughed. She still does have a sense of humor.

November, week 5
(ninety-nine weeks)

This was the first Thanksgiving in my entire life not spent with my mother—but that's not a bad thing; a little sad for me but not bad. It was her choice; I'm glad I asked and didn't just do. I went to her place while my turkey continued roasting, wondering if I would return with or without her. There were lots of residents there, so I didn't have to imagine her alone in a dining hall. Initially, I didn't find her, so I headed to her room. Not there. Then I heard her from down the hall—"Whoop-de-do!" ("woo-hoo" has morphed). She was looking especially festive sporting two strands of beads. She wanted me to leave my coat in her room—which, by the way, she remembered where it was.

She's always had a vain streak and never misses an opportunity to observe her reflection, so she noticed she didn't have lipstick on and immediately remedied that. Then we walked to the larger common area where she likes to introduce me to everyone—again and again. This was the best I've seen her in months. So I asked, "Do you want to have dinner here or come to my house for dinner?" Her simple response was "I'll eat here." She seemed relieved when I accepted her wishes. We sat for a while and visited; pretty much that involves me talking about random subjects and her grinning and nodding, occasionally interrupted by her announcing, "This is my daughter!" to any passersby.

Then it was time for me to leave, and she was very cordial and gave me two hugs and two kisses. She waved and said, "Bye-bye!" until I was out of her sight. She wasn't sad in the least; she didn't even ask when I would be back. She was where she felt comfortable and happy to be there.

November, week 4
(one hundred weeks)

Today, I supplied Mom with fun-size Milky Ways and Fudge Stripes cookies. She ate three fun-size bars as I was putting the treats away and kept urging me, "Help yourself!" I decided to get her away from the candy for a bit, so we ventured out to work on the community jigsaw puzzle.

We had to start a new puzzle and just worked around the fellow who was asleep at the table. We made fairly good progress when he awoke, made a nonsensical comment, to which I responded, "You bet," and then he began feeling around the puzzle pieces (which I had organized by color and theme—can we say "obsessive compulsive"?). Pretty soon, he sandwiched two puzzle pieces together and tried to take a bite. In that instant, I decided that I would pretend not to notice and assumed he would discover they weren't edible, until he turned them around and shoved them both in his mouth. I had to say something. I cautioned, "You don't want to eat those. They're puzzle pieces." He removed the saliva-covered pieces and placed them back in the mix. I avoided touching them and watched Mom like a hawk for the next half hour. I guess I've solved the mystery of missing puzzle pieces! Maybe they're good fiber.

December, week 1 (101 weeks)

Besides the "shoppers," there are the "wanderers" on the third floor. This small group seems to be intent to get somewhere; they just don't know where the somewhere is or why they need to be there. Often, they are rogue, but, occasionally, a couple will join together on their quest.

A new fellow moved in, and, at first, I wondered how he fit in this area. He was very pleasant, well dressed, and had an air of authority. Soon, I noticed that he was a wanderer and constantly trying doors, complaining that he couldn't do his job if he wasn't allowed access. I thought how sad, how frustrating to spend every waking minute trying to accomplish something that you never will.

December, week 2 (102 weeks)

It dawned on me that Mom hasn't asked about her checkbook in a couple of months. She also quit complaining about not having a car. She seems to either have forgotten about both or has accepted the fact of not having either.

I wish I could accept the facts of Mom's condition. I can tell myself all the right things, but, somehow, I can't feel it. I keep expecting Mom to act the way she used to. It disturbs me how I still have moments of impatience with her; they are not as often but will pop up on occasion. I know she does not remember things, and I also know when she is convinced of something, I won't be able to persuade her differently, yet often I get perturbed.

I've been working on my timing for visits, since I don't want to be a participant in the Sunday bingo game at Rosewood, just an observer. I make sure to arrive toward the end of the session. Today, I found Mom a winner (Oreo crumbs on her chest gave her away).

I noticed two of the residents playing bingo had bruises on their faces. I suppose they each had a fall, which happens fairly often. Then I began to imagine, what if they have gang activity on the third floor? Maybe there was as rumble or turf war, and those bruises Mom had the first week that she moved in may not have been from a fall but from being "jumped in" to a gang. The problem with that theory is they'd have trouble remembering which gang they were in.

Or maybe the facility was organizing fight nights. Can you picture that? Holding back the women in opposite corners with their walkers after you've enraged them over a staged bingo game incident.

December, week 3 (103 weeks)

On Christmas Eve, I arrived at my sister's, and who should emerge from the kitchen but my mother! I was unprepared for that. I had prepared, however, for the possibility of nostalgic sadness at experiencing another "first" without my mother. Karen and I had discussed the possibility of not including Mom this Christmas because she seems so anxious whenever she's taken from the facility. We tried conversation with Mom to get a feel of how she felt about the holidays, if she even recalled any. She has not reminisced about or even remembered any trips or events, nothing, in the past year. We came to no conclusions. Apparently, Karen decided to give it another try.

At six o'clock, just after dinner, Mom began the time announcements every five minutes. She expressed her desire to be going home by seven o'clock. There was no way that was going to happen; we had much more on our schedule. By a few minutes after seven, we were trying to get everyone in one room to distribute and open gifts. By five after, Mom was yelling up the stairs for the stragglers to "get down here!"

We finally succumbed to her displays of anxiety, and by seven thirty, we were brushing snow off the car and on the road by seven forty. Driving in a mini blizzard was a bit hairy, and the slow driving added time to the trip, which added to Mom's distress. We kept assuring her she'd get into the building without a problem.

Once inside, she had many more concerns; yes, she had a nightgown to sleep in, and, yes, she had a place to sleep, and, yes, we had cookies for her to snack on. We got her ready for bed and headed back to the family festivities.

My lesson from this: I just have to approach each day, special or nonevent, on an individual basis and wait to see how she's doing; forget planning anything ahead.

December, week 4
(104 weeks—two years)

In conversation, or at least an attempt at it, I asked if she had enjoyed being at Karen's for Christmas. Of course, she didn't recall Christmas at all. I see her eyes go up to the right trying to access a memory, but then they come back to focus on me, and she smiles, giggles a little, and says, "I don't even remember." I have to learn to quit trying to find something that is no longer there. It's not fair to her either; it's almost painful for her to try to recall.

As usual, when it was time for me to head out, she asked when I was coming back. That's funny because five minutes after I'm gone, she forgets I've been there, yet she wants to plan ahead. I answered my usual, "A couple of days." Since New Year's is coming up this week, I almost answered, "Next year," but I resisted. I think that was probably a good decision on my part.

January, week 1 (105 weeks)

I can't bring myself to go see Mom. The most devastating thing happened to me on New Year's Eve; my husband of forty years died suddenly. Other than diabetes and high blood pressure, he had no health issues, so this loss was a major shock. I'm still in a fog and imagine I will be for quite some time.

I don't plan on telling Mom of my loss; I know she won't comprehend it. I just don't want to visit Mom with this extreme emotional pain I'm experiencing and have to act as though all is well. Mom has forgotten Allen's name, but she recalls that I'm married, often asking when I prepare to leave if I'm going home to make dinner for my *hubby*. I'm afraid that question would make me cry. I don't expect sympathy from her because she's no longer capable of that emotion, but I *desire* for her to show compassion and put her arms around me, attempting to make it all better.

Karen understands and will keep me posted in regard to Mom. She has been a wonderful support for me. When I'm ready, she will accompany me to Mom's. I know Karen will patiently wait for me to be ready.

January, week 2 (106 weeks)

Karen told me that yesterday, Mom was quite disturbed about something "just terrible." She coerced an aide to accompany her to her apartment to check it out. There were numbers on her calendar! Go figure. The aide left Karen to sort this out with Mom. Since Mom realized her memory is suffering, she's been leaving herself notes on her calendar. The problem is they are too abbreviated to stimulate any memory, if in fact her memory can be stimulated at all. She pointed out 3-0-9, 3-0-9, 3-0-9. Karen told her that was her apartment number. Then she directed Karen to 9-2-0 on several days. It actually was written as a time, 9:20. I'm assuming that may have been a time she was administered medications. In her efforts to create memory, she's causing herself stress, convinced these numbers were important and there's some action required. Karen was unsuccessful in attempting to calm her, urging her to forget about it (now that's funny— memory problems and we suggest that she forget).

I think I will be able to visit Mom early next week. I will approach it as an escape from my thoughts and my grief; for an hour, I will attend to Mom and not talk or think about my loss.

I've made it a resolution for this New Year to try harder to learn patience. I'm not certain how to achieve that goal, but I've decided it wouldn't hurt to say a prayer on my way over to visit Mom.

January, week 3 (107 weeks)

Karen, Jillian, and I went to see Mom on Monday. Both Jillian and I had the day off work, and I was so happy to have her join us. It was a good visit, and, thankfully, Mom didn't ask about my hubby.

Mom was in rare form, even trying to joke with us a bit. The visit went so well that I decided to go again this week, solo.

I went on Saturday and found Mom very confused and obsessed about a baby that she thought I brought with me. She asked about the little children; when would they come back and which one was spending the night with her? I told her I was taking the baby home and the children would all be spending the night at their parents. It calms her when you enter her world and don't argue sense. Since she takes many little cat naps, maybe she dreams. She may have difficulty distinguishing between the dream and reality.

Possibly I've discovered the way I need to cope with her; rather than to be so intent with being right, I need to be more concerned with keeping her calm. Even when she's wrong, I'll let her win the argument. Now, finally, I understand what the dementia expert was saying. Why couldn't he just tell me this instead of repeating his three *don't* rules?

Since Mom was so disturbed by something she was imagining, I tried redirection. We moved from the apartment to the common area and tried working on the jigsaw puzzle. It was more like a job to her; she wanted to write it down when I found a piece that fit and kept asking what it was she was supposed to do. She was stacking the pieces in piles. I was amazingly patient with her (thank the Lord) and just let her do her thing; somehow, it made sense to her. She asked again what she was supposed to do, and I explained that there was nothing she *had* to do; it was *fun* taking all the pieces and putting them together to look like the picture on the box. Then she wanted the box. I thought maybe she was going to study the picture. Nope; she began putting all the pieces back in the box. The mess on the table disturbed her; so ended our activity together.

Meanwhile, the little lady from the corner apartment emerged every five minutes like a German cuckoo clock asking what time dinner was. She was anxious for dinner, yet she was still in her night clothes. She must not be paying for the next level of care including dressing assists.

Most of the time, I can't wait to leave that place and bask in the sane world. Fortunately, Mom enjoys short visits, appearing antsy after a half hour. When I can stretch it out to an hour, I think we're both beyond ready for the visit to end.

January, week 4 (108 weeks)

On Sunday, as I turned the corner to the hall heading toward Mom's apartment, I could hear her faint, desperate voice pleading, "Help me, please, please help me." I picked up the pace, and as I got closer, I realized she was attempting to engage two staffers to assist her with a jigsaw puzzle. Yes, she's back to the puzzles; however, she doesn't approach it as a fun, leisure-time activity; it's a job that must get done! Regardless, it keeps her busy, and, apparently, the aides too.

It turns out she had a urinary tract infection last week, and that's what added to her confusion. Lesson learned: don't assume it's the dementia progressing; consider it may be another stimulant and say something to someone. I felt bad that I noticed the increased confusion and allowed her to suffer for a couple of weeks.

February, week 1 (109 weeks)

Mom seems to be forgetting everyday words. She doesn't even struggle to recall a word any longer; she just replaces it (a rather *1984* Orwellian thing). The other day, a pocket was an envelope. Water, juice, coffee—they are all "liquids." At the very least, she is still capable of communicating.

She suffered a reaction to the antibiotic given her for the bladder infection and had a bout with diarrhea. Apparently, Mom can't recall the words "poop," "crap," and "shit." It is now referred to as "the brown stuff." This is descriptive; however, it could be used to substitute for beef gravy, baked beans, or chocolate anything.

February, week 2 (110 weeks)

Pretty much every time I visit, when Mom's not suffering bladder infection, she seems happy and introduces me to everyone, residents and aides alike. The introduction is vague, doesn't include my name, but she proudly announces to everyone that I'm her daughter. I don't know if she can't come up with my name, but I don't want to test her. I'm not sure I want to admit she's forgotten my name.

I've noticed there are things she used to say nearly every visit that she no longer has in her repertoire. Often, she would start the visit with "How was your week?" When it was time for me to head out, she used to ask if I was going home to my hubby. I'm grateful that she's not asking that question, as I am still quick to tears. Her final question was almost always when I was coming back.

Currently, her conversation is limited to asking where she lives.

February, week 3 (111 weeks)

I was suffering a terrible cold and stayed away from Mom's for several days. They don't want you visiting when you are ill, which makes perfect sense. I'm thankful for Karen, who visits a couple of times per week. When I can't get out to visit Mom, I rely on reports from Karen.

She shared with me that she answered Mom's phone while Mom was in the bathroom, and it was someone calling to verify a commitment to donate money to some organization. Karen told this person that there would be no donation and they were to take her number off their list.

We discussed possibly disconnecting the phone. Mom hasn't used it to call out in months. If solicitors continue to call, we could have problems. Mom is just too agreeable and wants to please everyone. Since we suspect she doesn't know how to dial the phone any longer, she won't miss it if we remove it.

February, week 4 (112 weeks)

I had happy family news to share with Mom. I informed her about my youngest son's, Pierce's, engagement to Missy. She smiled and commented that it was nice, but I'm certain she had no idea whom I was talking about. I tried to do some reminiscing about Pierce as a child and times that she babysat him. I said, "I remember when you took Phillip and Pierce overnight when they were seven and five, and they had such a great time with you." I went into extreme detail of the event. Then I brought up another memory that I had of her interaction with her grandsons. I was hoping to stimulate a memory but to no avail. She would smile, giggle, and make her "oh, really" comment, but she couldn't contribute to the tale or even admit to a recollection of anything. She did, however, appear to enjoy hearing the stories.

March, week 1 (113 weeks)

I'm thinking Mom seems more stressed when my sister and I are there together. She gets into that repetitive mode, pacing the small apartment and asking the same question every thirty seconds. Karen opened the closet to hang some clothes, and Mom suddenly became concerned about her nightwear. We tried to distract her with a cookie, but while she was chewing, she asked for the fifth time what was she going to sleep in. Then we distracted her with a candy bar. Again, within seconds, she was asking about her sleeping attire. At this rate, she soon won't fit in her nightgown! Obviously, the cookie/candy therapy is fruitless. We decided to distract her by getting her away from the closet, so we went for a walk (work off the cookie and candy bar). Then it was "Is this where I live? I don't know where my room is" every thirty seconds. I don't know why answering the same question over and over again is so exhausting, but it is.

March, week 2 (114 weeks)

We decided to disconnect the phone. It seemed silly to pay for something that gets absolutely no use. I removed it from Mom's room, and she never noticed.

I'm beginning to think the television is another item just taking up space. She doesn't appear to be interested in it. I contend that she can't follow a story line, so she loses interest quickly. One day, we found a polka program that kept her attention for a while, but that type of programming is difficult to find on a regular basis. Possibly something like a variety show might interest her, but I don't think she remembers how to turn the TV on or change channels.

She hasn't opened a Word-Find book in months. Rather than to occupy herself with working on a puzzle, she just sits and watches people. She also seems to be taking more cat naps. She continues to lose ground.

March, week 3 (115 weeks)

I ran out to Mom's yesterday and found her in pretty good spirits. My plan was to visit until the activity time, get her set up with that, and leave. She wanted no part of the activity unless I joined in. It was bingo. Do you have any idea how difficult it is to try and lose at bingo? I tried to not cover numbers that had been called, but my eagle-eyed mom was watching my card and kept correcting me. Before I knew it, Mom was yelling, "Bingo!" on my behalf. The residents do not like when an interloper wins; you're lucky to make it to the elevator in one piece with your winnings (a fun-size Snicker bar). The grumbling and stares are nearly unbearable! When it looked like I might win a second game, I just couldn't take it any longer and blamed the snow falling for my having to leave—quickly.

March, week 4 (116 weeks)

I got out to Mom's this morning but didn't time it very well. I ended up getting there too close to lunchtime. I avoid joining her for meals in memory care because it's just too depressing, but I thought it would be disturbing for her to have me rush out so quickly. I took a deep breath and asked if I could stay for lunch. There really is no conversation at the table; I just talk about anything I can think of, and she appears interested for a few moments and recites the appropriate response, like, "Oh, really?"

I told her about how sick my cat Willis had been and that I took him to the vet. He was diagnosed with thyroid disease, and I had to give him pills twice a day. I described how I hid the pill in cheese, and Willis ate it. Then the other lady at the table chimed in with a comment, "Wait until he goes to work and talks with his buddies, and they tell him about the cheese, then you'll have trouble." Thank God Willis doesn't have a job, much less buddies; nor can he speak—but, all that aside, I retorted, "Yes, you probably have a good point there." She must have missed the part about me taking Willis to the vet.

March, week 5 (117 weeks)

I couldn't find Mom today and started to get concerned. Then I checked the sign-out book and discovered she was down in the beauty salon. I found her asleep under the hair dryer. Conversation was especially difficult with the noise of the machine. I just kept making statements like "Willis is better" and "Karen's in Chicago," and Mom just kept saying, "What?" It was pretty unfulfilling, so she went to sleep again; shortest visit yet.

April, week 1 (118 weeks)

Today, I found Mom in the kitchen with a small group attempting conversation—the memory care version. She was offering a lady popcorn, but this woman couldn't settle in on the topic; she was busy in a conversation of her own that probably happened thirty years ago; I figured that out when she said she was expecting her mother for a visit. That was unlikely, as I surmise this woman was around ninety years old.

It was rather amusing to observe this coffee klatch; no one made much sense at all, yet they seemed to be enjoying each other. Beth, the aide, was so good with them. The woman who was expecting her mother wanted to call her, and Beth kept assuring they would do that after lunch. I expect after lunch she will amend that to "We'll call her after dinner."

I'm learning a lot from observing many of the aides in regard to handling the odd questions and repetition.

April, week 2 (119 weeks)

The other day, when I visited Mom, I found her in the common area, in front of the TV, on the edge of her seat, looking around and bouncing her feet up and down. Most everyone else was snoozing (I understand, as the program on the TV was describing how to draw in eyebrows). We took a little walk around, since she looked like she was preparing for a marathon. When we stopped in her apartment, she pointed out her jewelry, which she is very proud of. She is reduced to clip-on earrings, bangle bracelets, and beads that can go over her head because of her arthritic hands. The beads she is so fond of are, quality-wise, barely above those distributed at Mardi Gras (I just hope she hasn't "earned" them). It actually is very cute how she coordinates her jewelry with her outfits—it's like she's playing "dress-up." She loves the attention when someone comments on her jewelry, so I make sure to notice it each visit (actually, several times a visit—I too can play the repetition game).

April, week 3 (120 weeks)

I was preparing for a garage sale and found another box of my Mom's stuff in the garage. It was full of brand-new greeting cards. I looked through it and found quite the variety; get well, wedding, and mostly birthday. She was prepared for most everything. "Nice Girl" and "Nice Boy," several "Special Friend" birthdays, and ones for special ages—seventy, seventy-five, eighty, and one hundred. I don't know why that struck me funny.

April, week 4 (121 weeks)

When I visited Mom yesterday, I found her in the kitchen area enjoying coffee with my sister and brother-in-law. She was very pleasant, quite social; greeting everyone who passed by with a little wave and high-pitched "hello!" The next second, she was growling that no one was around, and she wanted hot coffee! Then she issued another loud "Hello" and wave, followed by the lower voice demanding more coffee. At that point, I wanted to ask if we could speak with "Louise" again, if this other personality would allow her to surface. Apparently, she had guzzled two cups already but forgot that. All she saw was an empty cup that needed rectifying.

We finally decided to move her away from the cup and took her down to her apartment. At that point, she wanted to write on her calendar a note that we had visited, but she couldn't find a pen. She was very impatient and annoyed and began swearing about the absence of writing implements. The flurry of curse words ended when Karen finally found a pencil. Whew! Strange visit.

May, week 1 (122 weeks)

I brought Mom a little goody bag with candy, pens, and lipsticks to replace ones the shoppers have absconded with. She read the Mother's Day card that accompanied the gift and said, "What a nice verse. I'm saving this," and put it back in the envelope. She checked out the goodies and ate a piece of candy. Then she opened the card, read it, and said, "What a nice verse. I'm saving this." This process repeated three more times.

May, week 2 (123 weeks)

While at Mom's, Beth, one of the aides, came in to her apartment to return her bangle bracelet and some earrings. She said she knew where the hot pink jewelry belonged.

Mom used to be good about locking her door. Now she forgets. Apparently, Karen and I are the only ones concerned about the shoppers who enter any unlocked door. Mom does not even notice anything is missing. Karen told me that one of Mom's angel figurines ended up in the dining room last week. I guess it's a good lesson to not have anything of value lying about.

I mentioned to Mom the importance of keeping her door locked, and she agreed, yet I don't expect her to comply. Talking with her feels so empty; she is always agreeable but can no longer contribute to conversation. I have been feeling lonely of late. I no longer have my mother to talk to about my husband. I no longer have my husband to talk to about my mother. I think I will call Karen and talk with her about both.

May, week 3 (124 weeks)

Karen and I visited Mom together this week. The doctor was giving her a routine check, and we wanted to be present. He asked her how old she was, and she answered that she was in her eighties, she couldn't remember exactly. When we told her eighty-eight, she was so surprised. He asked her to raise her arms (she had trouble last time because of a recent fall). This time, she raised them high above her head. She commented, "Not bad for being in my eighties," and asked again how old she was. We told her eighty-eight, and she was just as surprised as the first time we told her (two minutes earlier).

She was in a good mood. She had to tell everyone what wonderful daughters she has—several times.

May, week 4 (125 weeks)

I don't know if I will ever get used to the crazy at Mom's place. The one "shopper," wearing a pink hoodie, tied tight around her face, was standing in the hall gently rubbing a photo in another resident's shadow box (they're like address signs so people know where their room is), and was singing "God Bless America." A half hour later, when I left Mom's room, she was still rubbing and singing. How many verses are there to that song?

May, week 5 (126 weeks)

We're considering moving Mom into a companion suite. We had resisted this, assuming Mom would prefer her own space. They keep telling us that Mom suffers anxiety being alone. At night, she wants the aides to stay with her. They claim that often, when moved to a companion suite, residents make friends with their roommate and end up being inseparable, commenting how "cute" it is when the elderly women walk holding hands.

The cost to house Mom at Rosewood is an issue too. As she progresses in her "journey," she's requiring more services that add to the bill. A companion suite would cost much less and buy her more time here.

June, week 1 (127 weeks)

We made the decision to move Mom into the companion suite. We are hoping this will reduce her unease at being alone. This move will buy us more time financially; since she's very healthy, we may need more time.

Rosewood is a private pay care center and does not accept elderly waiver, which is a program for when the aged run out of funds. We may have to consider looking for a place that is not private pay within the year. Normally, you must prove to a new facility that you have funds for one to two years before applying for elderly waiver. We're all right for now, but it is something we'll have to consider for the not-too-distant future. I have to pay close attention to her finances so that we don't deplete her funds to the point of requiring aid.

I hoped she might be able to spend the rest of her days here. That may not be the case.

June, week 2 (128 weeks)

We had a choice of two rooms to move Mom into. The one we selected opened near the kitchen/dining/activity area. We felt that would give Mom some comfort.

We're in a wait-and-see mode with the new room. I thought it would solve problems; now I'm not sure. We were told she could keep the door shut, locked if she wanted. She often forgets to lock it, but she definitely wants it closed. An open door is an invitation to the shoppers. Now we're told it has to stay open because her roommate is a fall risk. They'll have a battle with Mom if they try to reason with her and expect her to remember. Don't they know they're dealing with memory care residents? My intent was to find her some peace, not create a new stress. I will be talking with them.

June, week 3 (129 weeks)

I finally heard from the director at Mom's, and she assured me the situation with Mom will have her best interests at the forefront. I was quite annoyed that I hadn't heard back in a timely manner, but, apparently, my mother is not the only one who confuses me and my sister. Karen visited the other day, and the director gave her the answer to my question. Apparently, the aide who told us the door had to remain open was in error. It makes me much more comfortable with the move.

Again, we haven't told Mom about the change. Rosewood will physically move all her furniture and belongings. They will do this while she is busy with an activity. Since she cannot remember where her room is, she may not notice. We don't make a big deal about things, and she just rolls with it all, probably assuming it's always been as it is now.

The new room is much smaller. It was a single-person unit that they changed to a two-person suite. We remember this room from the initial tour of the facility. They seem to pretend not to know this fact. The area that will be Mom's bedroom was originally the small living room, more like an entryway. The window to the outside is in the roommate's bedroom. There is a window in Mom's room, but it looks out to the hallway.

I hope we made the right decision. I don't like how small the room is and that there is no window for Mom to look outside, something she likes to do. We will give up her TV, dining set, and rocker, since there is no room for them.

I feel tremendously sad. I'm still dealing with my grief and would like something, anything to run smoothly. Somehow, I don't feel equipped to handle important decisions.

June, week 4 (130 weeks)

Rosewood moved Mom into her new room. We didn't tell her she was moving down the hall. All her pictures and angels were displayed, and it looked familiar. Since she never remembered where her initial room was, we hoped she would just accept this new room as the place she had always been.

She was curious about the person in the other room. We told her it was her roommate, which she accepted.

We moved the small refrigerator into the new room, since we like to keep it stocked with juice and snacks. Mom doesn't realize it houses food. It has a door that conceals the contents, so as far as she's concerned, it's a large white square statue.

July, week 1 (131 weeks)

I'm still trying to justify moving Mom to the companion suite. I didn't anticipate that the move would disturb me so much. I try to convince myself that she will be less anxious knowing there is someone in the next room. That's what they told us would happen. I tell myself that she won't miss the larger apartment because she continually forgets that she lives there. She doesn't have the memory of the nicer unit, so how can she miss it?

I'm failing in my rationalizations.

July, week 2 (132 weeks)

As expected, Mom has accepted her room as though she has always been there. She voices no complaints. Regardless, I still have this feeling that I've done her an injustice.

Today, I took a ride on the verbal merry-go-round with her. We went with a group down to the first floor for entertainment, a military ensemble providing music. "What floor is this? What floor do I live on? Where's my room? What are we doing? What floor is this? What floor do I live on?" And round and round we went. I got off the ride after about twenty minutes, just as they were preparing to sing. I hope Mom enjoyed the program. I hope she was able to shut up for a while so others could enjoy the program.

July, week 3 (133 weeks)

We noticed the empty bed in the other room of Mom's companion suite. Initially, there was a woman asleep in it. The bed wasn't made up; blankets and sheets were folded neatly in piles. It was confirmed Mom's roommate is in the hospital. Mom is back to being alone every night (in a much smaller area than she previously enjoyed).

Mom likes to walk into her roommate's room to look out the window. I feel badly that we chose this room that doesn't have a window to the outside. Our only consolation is that she doesn't spend much time in her room. She is normally only there to sleep.

July, week 4 (134 weeks)

I had a busy day today, lunch at work with friends, and then was waiting at home for a service call, which came early in the four-hour window. That gave me the time to run out and visit Mom. She was thrilled to see me and paraded me through the kitchen to tell everyone, "This is my daughter." When one resident asked her what she had named me, she couldn't remember. I quickly helped her out, and Mom added, "That's right, Karen and Maggie."

Mom asked if I knew where her room was. I showed her, and we entered; she wanted me to open every drawer so I could see all her stuff. That surprised me because, normally, she doesn't seem to understand drawers, cupboards, or closets. She was especially proud of her jewelry hung on the three jewelry trees on top of her dresser. There was a tray with compartments that held her earrings that she pawed through to show me the ones with the most sparkle.

We then headed down to the puzzle table and worked on one that was half done. We challenged each other to find pieces and laughed with every accomplishment. It felt so good to laugh with her. I found myself wishing I could share my troubles with her and ask her advice, but those days are gone.

Wanting to be ahead of rush-hour traffic, I told her I needed to head out. At first, she seemed surprised, stating, "Oh, you don't stay here?" She accepted my answer and then wanted to walk me to the elevator, and after several kisses and "I love you" statements, I got on the elevator as she repeated, "Bye-bye," until the door closed.

I'm glad I found the time to visit. Her expressions of joy today relieved my feelings of guilt.

August, week 1 (135 weeks)

I've heard it said that people with dementia are childlike, and I agree that often they *act* childlike. The difference is that a child has potential; there is capability for them to learn; they learn from example and correction. Dementia patients don't have that potential; they will only continue to degrade.

I had a brief visit with Mom today. My litmus test of a jigsaw puzzle proved her to be somewhat confused but not extreme. The puzzle had the entire border completed but not much progress in the center. Mom selected one piece and became irritated when it wouldn't fit anywhere she tried; zero to frustration in two seconds. She verged on a tantrum, loudly swearing, which is so out of character for her. When I found a piece and gave it to her and then pointed to an area it probably belonged, she could place it right off and was very pleased with herself. Today, she just needed a little more help. I think my patience level is improving.

August, week 2 (136 weeks)

The original roommate never returned from the hospital, but they didn't waste much time filling the room. Mom asks practically every time I visit who the other person in her room is. My answer is always the same, and she accepts it.

The other resident is almost always in bed. When she's not sleeping, if she is wheeled out of her room, she carries a doll that everyone refers to as Michael. Mom may have a horrible memory, but she still has one foot in the real world.

I don't suspect there is much hope that Mom and her roommate will become friends. The cute story they told us about elderly roommates becoming best friends isn't going to happen for Mom.

August, week 3 (137 weeks)

I found Mom in the kitchen area where they had just finished a bingo game. That was great timing on my part—I hate joining in because residents don't like when outsiders win, and Mom won't let me cheat to lose. After I sat down, a woman asked who I was, and I answered quickly before Mom could interpret the question as a test. I hate when some of the aides will ask Mom, "Who's here to visit you?" Even seemingly simple questions cause her stress, forcing her to attempt to recall something she may not have access to. You would think they would know that.

Within a few minutes, Mom pointed to a green door and asked if that was the restroom. I was impressed she remembered the color coding (all restrooms on the third floor have a green door). She asked if I wanted to accompany her, to which I replied that I would wait in the hall. After a short time, she emerged and headed a different direction; she had forgotten I was there. I grabbed my stuff and ran after her, surprising her again. I let her think I just got there. What's the point of correction?

When I left, she wanted to know when I was coming back. I always answer, "A couple of days," because she won't know tomorrow from next week, and she's happy with the answer.

August, week 4 (138 weeks)

While sitting with Mom, waiting for an activity to begin, I started to have a conversation with another resident, Elaine. It seemed pretty normal, and she's very pleasant. She asked how Mom and I were related. We talked for a few minutes, and then she asked how Mom and I were related; silly me, so much for a normal conversation.

Then poor Elaine became fixated on the whereabouts of her husband, and the aides would answer, "He's in heaven." Honestly, I think I would have answered, "He's down the hall." What horrible news to get every five minutes. Pretty soon, she began crying, and my heart just broke for her. She didn't know who she was, where she was, or where she was supposed to be. The aide told her that her name was Elaine and gave her several options of places to be and things to do. Then she offered her a cookie. The tears immediately stopped, and she was very pleased to have a cookie. Ahh, the underestimated power of the cookie.

August, week 5 (139 weeks)

Today, Mom slept through the entire visit, sitting in a chair. She awoke for seconds at a time to grin at me and say, "It's so good to see you." Then she'd drop off to sleep again. I woke her about a half-dozen times to make inane conversational statements. I finally let her sleep about fifteen minutes and watched *Bonanza* (can't believe I used to enjoy that show—how stupid it seems now).

Mom has always had trouble sleeping at night. I wonder if she had experienced a bad night and that was why she was so tired. I woke her to say good-bye. She grinned and said, "OK." At least she was dressed, had her beads, earrings, and lipstick on, and was sitting in the common area, unlike her roommate who spends every moment in bed now with Michael tucked near her.

September, week 1 (140 weeks)

My sister noticed Mom's pillow was missing the other day and asked an aide. The aide said she knew where it was; Mom had slept in a different room the night before. Karen asked if that happened often, wondering if Mom was instigating her own sleepovers. Apparently, her roommate was in hospice, and family had been called. I suppose it was better to move Mom for a night rather than to subject her to the momentary trauma (everything is momentary for Mom these days).

We moved Mom into a companion suite two months ago to provide her the comfort of having someone near since she had become fearful of being alone. In two months, two roommates have died. I am hoping that the next roommate will have some degree of longevity.

September, week 2 (141 weeks)

We planned another celebration for Mom's eighty-ninth birthday with a lunch on the first floor for the family.

I initially went up to Mom's room to get her and found Karen and Jillian were already there. Mom kept calling my sister "Mom" and asked who I was. She may have been confused because Jillian was there; therefore, in her mind, I was accounted for. When she asked, "Who are you?" we laughed, thinking she was making a joke. She laughed too and then added, "No, really, who are you?" When I told her, she looked puzzled, probably trying to compute why there was two of me. We decided to shift gears and took her down to the gathering.

It was a nice party. Mom announced birthdays are good because you get presents. It's difficult to buy gifts for her because she needs nothing. She got some socks and a bracelet. One of the great grandsons drew a picture for her. My son Phillip put together a small photo album of his family and put the names in large print on every picture. I thought that was very clever.

September, week 3 (142 weeks)

I wish we had been faster and suggested moving Mom to the other side of the companion suite after the last roommate passed. They very quickly moved another woman in, but, again, I'm not expecting that a friendship will develop. It appears this one is another who spends the majority of her day in bed.

Maybe I shouldn't think this way, but I'm beginning to wonder if it's all about money. When we moved Mom into Rosewood initially, they were offering a move-in special of reduced rent. Moving Mom out of her apartment allowed them to move someone in at the higher rate. The fact that this new room was originally a one-person unit, now housing two, provides them even more money. They haven't offered us the other half when it's been available twice. That makes me wonder if they've negotiated more money for that area.

Another disturbing issue arose. Karen noticed a blanket on the floor on one side of the bed. When she picked it up, she noticed it was heavily weighted on two sides. It appeared to be a form of restraint. We've been told that Mom tends to be up often during the night and will wander. However, restraints are illegal. Karen told Mom's doctor about what she found, but we didn't approach Rosewood in regard to it. We have an abnormal aversion to confrontation, and we didn't expect them to give us a truthful answer anyway.

I'm really thinking it may be time to look elsewhere. I can see the end of her money on the horizon; it's distant yet, but it's visible. I feel manipulated. I'm becoming concerned with how they are handling my mother. Mostly, I cannot rationalize away the dismal closet we call her room.

September, week 4 (143 weeks)

I stopped by to see Mom this afternoon, and I noticed she was wearing slippers. I asked to see her toes because she had been complaining about pain from a corn. I wanted to check to see if they had applied the corn pads I brought last week, but I also wanted to check out the bottom of the slippers to be sure they weren't slick. They did have a slight tread, which is good. However, no corn pad, so we went to her room to rectify that. I found the pads immediately; first top drawer, just where I showed the aide I put them; they claimed they couldn't find them.

When we headed back out to the living room, I couldn't help but notice a resident struggling to take steps with her walker. She had brand-new running shoes on, the kind with lots of raised tread, heel to toe. They're probably tremendous for the Olympic track, but for the ninety-year-old shuffle, they are quite dangerous. What was her family thinking when they bought these shoes? *Oh, Grandma will look so cute in her trendy shoes.* Yeah, until she falls and breaks a hip! And what about the aide who helped her dress this morning? Don't they know whom they're caring for? Old people don't lift their feet; they can't. I was just about to run over to help her when one of the aides came to the rescue and assisted her into her room (I hope to change her shoes). I didn't see her again before I left.

October, week 1 (144 weeks)

They had an activity in the kitchen that I urged Mom to join. It's called the cooking club, which is pretty much any residents who can follow instructions. They were baking muffins from a just-add-water mix. Residents are seated around a large table, and an aide instructs them on what to do. One woman's job was to place the liners in the pans. Another fellow poured the water in after the woman to his left had dumped the mix in the bowl. Then the aide pushed the bowl in front of Mom and asked her to stir. She defiantly announced, "I'm not going to stir it!" So the aide passed it to the next woman, who glanced at Mom and then back at the bowl and stated, "I'm not going to stir it!" And so it went around the entire table, the whole group refusing to stir. Mom started a revolution! Viva Louise!

October, week 2 (145 weeks)

One of the activities they involve the residents in is art projects. This week, Mom had a collage of bright tissue glued on a square of cardboard representing leaves on a tree. I complimented her on her artwork, but she didn't recall creating it.

In her younger years, she was quite artistic. There was a pencil drawing she had done of Carmen Miranda that was stunning. She never pursued her drawing talent. She expressed her artistic gifts with sewing and cooking, more substantial areas. She sewed most of our clothes, and they looked store-bought. Desserts she created looked like photos from magazines. When she entertained, the table she set was a work of art.

The tissue tree she designed at the home indicated to me that she still had her sense of the artistic. She didn't remember doing the project, but I'm sure she enjoyed creating it at the moment.

October, week 3 (146 weeks)

I raced to get to Mom's for her one-thirty doctor appointment. Then I sat with her for an hour waiting for the doctor.

With the exception of the three wanderers, the residents were all seated in front of the TV lost in 1955 watching Lucy and Desi. Then one of the wanderers approached the TV and began to fiddle with the remote. Once the screen went to blue, she walked away. Everyone continued to watch the blue screen (including me) until, finally, someone ordered another wanderer to put it back to where it was. He got quite upset that it wasn't his fault and said, "The other guy took it." I'm not sure what that meant, as it was a woman who caused the initial problem and she left with nothing. Finally, an aide appeared and fixed the issue, mere moments before a true uprising.

I observed for a full hour the run of the mill on the third floor. The three wanderers were residents on a mission. Their mission could be twenty or thirty years old, but they are dedicated to it. Occasionally, they would approach someone, anyone, and make a statement of pure nonsense. They make circles around the floor, intersecting on occasion. Finally, two of them joined forces and attempted to assist the other in their quest. The third one is too busy pocketing any items that would fit in her jacket (she's the best of the shoppers). The TV interrupter wanted me to find the postman; I couldn't help her out. After she leaned into me with her hand on my knee and tears in her eyes, stating, "He's got the brown platter," I could take no more. I responded, "OK," and headed off to find someone who might be able to contact the doctor and find out when he was coming. I found out he will be there tomorrow at one thirty; apparently, I had the appointment wrong.

I'm looking forward to tomorrow!

October, week 4 (147 weeks)

I found out that Mom went on an outing the other day. The van took residents to a play, and Mom went with her new best friend, Lily. We didn't know anything about Lily, but, apparently, they dine together and sit by each other during activities. Lily is new to the building and seems to be very social. They must have noticed that trait in each other and became instant buddies. I can't imagine that Mom offers much to the friendship other than smiles, but it's nice to know she has a friend.

November, week 1 (148 weeks)

I visited Mom today after a four-day mini vacation to Laughlin, Nevada. I didn't tell her I was going because she would forget, and why cause her the distress for even a few minutes? She doesn't like when we're gone.

While I was there, I stepped out of her sight a couple of times, and each time I returned, she was surprised to see me, saying, "Oh, Maggie! It's so good to see you!" So, basically, I awarded her three surprise visits today. I made up for the days I was gone and made her very happy times three. She made me happy by recalling my name three times.

November, week 2 (149 weeks)

Walking into the lobby of the facility, you will find a bulletin board with pictures of residents making crafts or involved in an activity or attending events. There is also a section where, should there be a loss, a picture of the departed resident is posted with their name and dates of birth and passing. I felt a twinge of shock, followed by sadness when I noticed the picture of Lily. I had only met her the one time, but in her short stay, she had been a friend to Mom, and I appreciated that.

When I went up to the third floor, I found Mom sitting in the common area. I approached her and said, "I'll bet you're going to miss Lily." She responded, "Who's Lily?"

November, week 3 (150 weeks)

I've been nursing a cold for a week and therefore haven't dared visit Mom. I have felt horribly guilty even though I know staying away is the right thing to do.

My sister called to check on me today, and I told her I haven't been able to visit Mom. She visited her yesterday, and Mom told her I had just been there, that Karen just missed me. Funny, that took care of my guilt feelings.

November, week 4 (151 weeks)

My sister, Karen, is such a good caregiver to Mom. Being retired, she has the time to visit Mom often, and I'm grateful for that.

I talked with Karen today and got an update. Karen had encouraged Mom to try to go to the bathroom (we don't want her dependent on adult diapers). She had given Mom a piece of cheese, which she was holding while waiting on nature. Karen noticed Mom's skin was dry, commenting that they needed to lotion up her legs, and turned away to get some lotion. Karen admitted that she had issued too many instructions back to back; when she turned around to Mom, she was rubbing the cheese slice on her leg. Who knows, maybe she discovered a new moisturizer—cheese. Hopefully, they won't let the house dog on the third floor. I can picture this golden retriever dragging Mom across the floor by her cheese-covered leg. I hope today is bath day.

November, week 5 (152 weeks)

I finally got out to visit Mom today; I have no indications of having had a cold. Normally, she will say that I haven't been there in "so long" even if it's only been a day or two. This time, because of my cold, I had a really good excuse, but she didn't make her usual statement. I'm not sure if she recognized me today.

We checked out the jigsaw puzzle, but it didn't go well. She labored over one piece trying to make it fit, but where she wanted it to go was on an edge, and it was not an edge piece.

Pretty soon, I overheard an aide asking another resident if she wanted to hear accordion music. I perked up because Mom used to play piano accompaniment to her sister's accordion playing. I suggested Mom join the group. She appeared eager to do so. We took the elevator to the first floor, and I watched Mom's excitement turn into anxiety; she often gets uncomfortable when she leaves the third floor. I got her set up in a chair facing the musician, who had already begun to play. I whispered to Mom that I would be heading out and added, "I love you." She didn't respond; she looked irritated. Then she very loudly, so the entire first floor could hear, asked, "What the hell am I doing here?" I shushed her and whispered that she was listening to accordion music—"Isn't that nice?" She did not look happy about it. I left. I hope she managed to sit through the rest of the performance without incident. I guess I'll cross another thing off the list of things I thought Mom would enjoy.

December, week 1 (153 weeks)

I'm coming to the realization that each day is a new day with Mom. One day, she will remember my name, and the next time I see her, she has that look like she's trying to recall from where she knows me. One day, she is all smiles and keeps saying that it's so good to see me, and the next day, she's irritated and anxious, cursing over something minor. I find that after a good visit, I tend to expect the next one to be a carbon copy, and then I'm disappointed. I guess I should be thankful that she recognizes me more often than not.

December, week 2 (154 weeks)

Today, I found Mom in the common area watching a Russian orchestral program on the TV; not really my cup of tea, but I decided to enjoy it with her, since conversation suffers so terribly between us these days. It wasn't awful; they were playing a faintly familiar Russian tune. Then two of the wanderers sat down, and the gentleman began to sing along, except he wasn't singing the same tune. He was singing "A Few of My Favorite Things." The woman who often wanders with him began to sing along too—a completely different song that I couldn't distinguish. Shortly, the man forgot what his favorite things were and began whistling. The woman continued to sing and hum. To say the least, it was pretty disruptive. I kept reminding myself that these were people not of sound mind, and I should just try to tune them out. Fortunately, they were mysteriously stimulated to wander again, and the woman began her journey. The man followed but only after taking sections of the newspaper and placing them about the sofa and chair. Mom was curious as to what he was doing. That was pretty much our only conversation of the afternoon, and I couldn't give her an explanation. At that point, the beautician appeared; it was Mom's turn in the salon. This was my opportunity to say my farewell and give Mom a kiss good-bye.

All the way home (and at this very moment), I had the "Favorite Things" melody repeating in my head! ". . . And whiskers on kittens . . ."

December, week 3 (155 weeks)

Christmas Eve this year is at my house. The kids approached me and suggested I not try to bring Grandma home. They cited how anxious she was last year. Somehow, Karen and I ignored her anxiety; either that or we're so used to it, we don't notice it as others do. The main issue should be Mom's comfort. I really debated over my decision but finally came to the conclusion that I wanted her there for my sake, not hers. I felt guilty not including her, but I have to remember that she's not who she was even a few years ago. In reality, she won't know Christmas from any other day.

December, week 4
(156 weeks—three years)

I found Mom in good spirits, and, today, I think she knew who I was, unlike Christmas Day when she acted happy to see me, but within moments, I realized she didn't have a clue who I was. I guess she was just happy to have company.

What made the visit brutal was watching an Elvis movie (*Kismet*) that didn't even make a B-movie list (possibly an F). For some reason, Mom seemed intent on watching it. That was odd, as, lately, she seems to lack the focus to follow a program on TV. As Elvis climbed over a wall in his brightly colored silk vest and balloon pants, Mom laughed with delight.

It was difficult to get much out of the movie, since one of the male residents was busy entertaining three ladies. He would authoritatively make random statements that didn't link together in any sense, and the ladies would giggle and look at each other. One would occasionally comment, but it made just about as much sense as his rambling. Then he began to clap loudly and give instruction while performing this amazing act. That annoyed a fellow trying to read the paper, who yelled at him to "knock it off!" The clapping man apologized and added that he was just doing his job. He claimed to have received a call and was asked to clean it up, so that's what he was doing. The response from the newspaper-reading man was a loud "You're an asshole!" I was bracing for a knock-down-drag-out fight, and then I realized most of the residents aren't ambulatory, and that was probably not an option. It quickly wound down to mumbling, and the clapper wandered away, complaining it wasn't his job, and the kids should do it 'cause *he wasn't going to do it*. Mom missed the entire altercation because she had fallen asleep. I woke her to tell her I was heading out.

January, week 1 (157 weeks)

Mom called me at home last night using an aide's phone. She's never done that before. I imagine she had exhausted the patience of the aide with her concern, and the aide suggested she call me. Mom was concerned about the children that were there. She didn't think it was right that they should stay with her overnight. I realized shortly into the conversation that she truly believed there were children in her room, so I told her it was all right because the parents were on their way to come get them. She accepted that response and sounded relieved.

Sometimes you just have to play along.

I think Mom may have a little spark of memory in regard to the three of us traveling. She often thinks she's at a hotel. Today, she wanted to get her purse to take with her and had a sweater and slippers. We told her she didn't need these items, but she insisted on the purse. She literally growled, "I'm taking it!"

I felt bad that she thought we were going on an outing. I felt like we disappointed her. Thankfully, she forgot about it quickly.

Mom used to insist on having her purse with her at all times. We had long ago taken anything important out of it. Her identification, medical cards, and Social Security card were moved to a safe in my house. She got used to not having any money in her wallet even though she would occasionally ask you what she owed you if you gave her something like a cup of coffee or a candy bar.

Now she randomly carries a purse depending on her mood. Today, she was in one of those moods.

January, week 2 (158 weeks)

My sister and I had a "care conference" today at Mom's. I arrived first to find her standing in the hallway and made the mistake of asking why she was standing there. She shrugged her shoulders and said, "I don't know," and then yelled in an angry voice, "Where am I supposed to be?" I hushed her; she surprised me with her hollering. I suggested we go in her room.

Then Karen showed up. Mom's demeanor changed; she was so happy and gave us each big hugs and told us she loved us. Karen put her supplies away, and I used the restroom. When I came out, Mom was so surprised to see me. I got another big hug and kiss.

We set Mom up for lunch in the dining room and told her we would be right back. We met with the nurse and learned that Mom has been swearing a lot lately, especially at bingo. Other than that, she is doing well. I wasn't sure what they wanted us to do about the swearing; it's obvious correction doesn't stick.

Later, after the conference, we saw that Mom was involved in a group activity—well, the rest of the group was actively listening to the presenter of a slide show; Mom was sleeping. We decided to head out without waking her.

On the ride home, we talked about things from the past that were probably indications of dementia before we realized it. Mom's falling asleep in the middle of the activity reminded us of the time Mom had invited us to a mother-daughter event at her church. They had a women's speaker, and Mom had secured three seats in the front row. As soon as the speaker opened her mouth, Mom fell asleep. We were on either side of her and took turns elbowing her to wake her. We were so embarrassed. The speaker was only ten or fifteen feet in front of us, and we were certain she had to notice Mom snoozing away. After the event, we chastised Mom relentlessly for being so rude. Mom didn't respond; she just slightly shrugged her shoulders. Karen and I agreed that we could have been a lot less intense with Mom after that episode. We talked about how we individually and together reprimanded Mom often in the couple of years before her diagnosis. We were not proud of ourselves.

January, week 3 (159 weeks)

Apparently, Mom's glasses went missing for a few days. Then Karen noticed them on someone else's face. She pointed it out to an aide. That aide approached the resident and took the glasses, saying she was going to clean them, and then returned them to the rightful owner. I'm so glad Mom doesn't wear dentures.

January, week 4 (160 weeks)

I put off visiting Mom for as long as I could (the last visit she slept through), and the guilt began to set in. I had time today, so I made the trip this morning. I've had some difficulty getting myself motivated of late. I blame it on the grief.

I found Mom alert and talkative. She informed me someone told her she was going to style her hair. She obviously had just returned from the salon with a new haircut and every sparkling white hair in place.

She was annoyed that the blinds were down in the common area and she couldn't see outside, so I fixed that. I had a familiar twinge of guilt in regard to the room we picked for her with no outside window.

Then I complimented her on her bracelet (a Christmas gift from my son Pierce—large, wide piece of bling with lots of faux gems). She proudly announced, "I made it." I didn't correct her. I just told her she did a really nice job and she should make more. I suggested we could sell them at Kohl's (calling them Apt 9).

January, week 5 (161 weeks)

Acknowledging how I should react and feel and actually feeling it seem to be two different things. I can rationalize understanding and acceptance, but I can't yet feel it. I still have moments of irritation and times of resentment. I find it so hard to get in the car with the intention of visiting Mom. I'd much rather go shopping. I hope someday to actually want to go see her. I feel right now I'm doing it out of some sense of loyalty. I force myself to make the weekly trip to spend thirty to sixty minutes with my mother. I feel very guilty about my attitude.

February, week 1 (162 weeks)

I find that I am looking for excuses to delay my visits with Mom. I look for any justification. It's too cold out. I think I saw a snowflake fall. Oh my god, I sneezed; maybe I'm catching a cold.

I remember a time when I was talking to a neighbor about church. I admitted that I didn't often attend because I didn't feel I got much out of it. She recommended I attend on Sunday with a different purpose. Go, not to expect anything for yourself, but go to worship God. That intrigued me, and I tried it that Sunday. I was amazed at what I got out of the service when I changed my attitude.

As Debra told me months ago, "It's not all about you." I guess I need to change my attitude in regard to my visits with Mom. I've been focusing on how depressing or tense the visit can be for me or how sad I feel when she doesn't recognize me. Instead, I should go because it makes her happy. Even when she doesn't recognize me, she's happy to have a visitor.

February, week 2 (163 weeks)

Shortly after I arrived at Mom's and sat down next to her in the common area, she got up. I asked if she wanted to take a walk, which we did. She doesn't often suggest things to do, so this was refreshing. We came across the table by the shelf of jigsaw puzzles. I pulled one out, and we began. She nearly single-handedly built the entire frame. With each piece that fit into another, she exclaimed, "Woo-hoo!"

Before the puzzle was done, the entertainment arrived, providing me my opportunity to bug out. A lady was going to play the piano for the group, so I moved Mom to a chair where she could see the pianist better.

Mom let me give her a kiss, not pulling back with the "Who are you?" look on her face. She wanted to know when I'd be back. I said, "A couple of days," and she moaned, so I changed it to "Maybe tomorrow. We'll see how it goes." As I headed down the hall, she waved and said, "Bye-bye! Bye-bye!"

I went with no expectations, and I was pleasantly surprised with what I found.

February, week 3 (164 weeks)

I had been visiting with Mom for about twenty minutes when the aides began collecting some residents for a project, so I escorted Mom into the activity area. They were going to do a service project. Really? They *are* the service project! They were going to make fleece blankets for an animal rescue, for critters waiting to be adopted. Maybe it's me, but giving scissors to this group is like giving scissors to a preschool class. I decided not to witness the carnage and gave Mom my farewells. I expect next time I visit, she may have a new hairstyle.

February, week 4 (165 weeks)

This week, when I visited Mom, I found her playing bingo. She is the unofficial, self-declared bingo cop. Dora, who spent the first few minutes of the game attempting to grind G-53 into oblivion with her fork, had lost the concept of the game and simply filled her card with the poker chips. This drove Mom absolutely bonkers. She was quite loud announcing that those numbers weren't called. When an aide told her that it was all right, she disagreed! She was often distracted by Elaine, to her left, who was a slow to notice that she had the called number. Mom would become very animated, pointing at her card, and in a loud, obviously annoyed voice, yell at her, "You got that, N-45!" repeating it until Elaine finally managed to cover it. Tons of fun at the home! By the time I left, I had the jitters. I think I've acquired a tick.

March, week 1 (166 weeks)

I was surprised to find a paper cup with pills in it on Mom's dresser. I brought them to the nurses' station and said, "I found these pills in my mother's room." The answer I got back was "I didn't do it." That caught me off guard. I expected some sort of apologetic response, not a defensive one.

My problem is that I back off way too easily. It is my nature not to provoke. When things move away from cordial, I shut down. Maybe it's my fear that I will react with tears that causes me to avoid any type of confrontation.

This incident bothered me. Not only did Mom probably miss some doses of medication, but also the staff didn't seem to care. I should have pursued it; at very least, I should have complained to the management. Instead, I find I'm beating myself up for my inaction.

March, week 2 (167 weeks)

Mom is adversely attracted to people who carry extra weight. She likes to point out big bellies and butts. Today, she noticed an aide who was quite large. She's not very quiet about it, displaying her obvious lack of filters. The thing is that she forgets that she noticed her and, ten seconds later, discovers her again and repeats her announcement. I felt bad for the poor overweight aide who had to hear this comment of disdain several times. She was facilitating a sing-along and couldn't just walk away; she had to continue and suffer insults every few seconds. I couldn't even remove Mom from the area because she loves the sing-alongs and refused to leave.

This should serve as my incentive to not gain any more weight!

March, week 3 (168 weeks)

Today, I sat with Mom in the common area and participated in exercises with her for a few minutes. Shortly after the session was over, they began organizing the more-alert residents for an outing to a restaurant for lunch. Again, I didn't want Mom to miss this event to spend a half hour with me; we can kill time another day. I urged her to go and rode down the elevator with her and another ten folks. The whole time, she made happy exclamations. "Woo-hoo! Whoop-de-do!" I walked with her to the bus, but when she was supposed to get on, she became agitated and protested, "I want to be with my daughter!" I soothed her by telling her that I couldn't go with them, but I'd come back. I told her to go and have a good time. She relaxed and got on the bus (she wanted to sit in the driver's seat). I repeated that I would come back, which wasn't exactly a lie; it just wouldn't be this day. I know that two minutes after she was on the bus, she would have forgotten I was there at all. It still made me feel sad.

She certainly lives in the moment these days. We're not making memories anymore, so my focus needs to be on giving her happy moments.

March, week 4 (169 weeks)

After I set Mom up in the kitchen with the cooking club, I went back to her room to use her restroom. When I came out, I could hear Mom saying, "No!" I stood by the hallway window to the kitchen and watched an aide attempting to move Mom's walker. Mom is extremely possessive over her walker and demands it be near her at all times. At this time, the walker was not in the way or taking up a spot for another resident. It appeared to me to be a war of wills between Mom and the aide. The aide would try to pull it away, but Mom had a white-fisted grip on it. I was curious to see if this would escalate, so I watched on until the aide looked up and noticed me. She quickly released the walker and moved away.

I went into the kitchen and joined Mom, who was trying to drink her coffee while holding tight to the walker. The problem was that her arm holding the walker crossed over her arm with the coffee cup. She wanted to sip the coffee but couldn't get the cup close to her mouth. I showed Mom that we could take the beads she had hanging on her walker (to distinguish it from other walkers) and wrap them around the arm of the chair; therefore, no one would take it. She relaxed, let go of the walker, and sipped her coffee. She was happy with my solution.

I've decided to watch this particular aide and her interaction with residents. Her stubbornness seemed inappropriate to me.

April, week 1 (170 weeks)

Karen went to visit Mom last week, and when she got off the elevator, she was met by one of the aides who shared that Mom was "on the warpath" because they had all her bras in the laundry. Karen found Mom in a common area working on a jigsaw puzzle. When she greeted her, Mom placed both palms under breasts (which gravity had claimed years ago) and jogged them rapidly up and down, exclaiming, "Look at this! I don't have a bra! How does this happen!" It wasn't until they brought the laundered and dried bras and let Mom put one on that she totally calmed down.

Lesson: do not mess with a dementia patient's routine.

April, week 2 (171 weeks)

Mom is very cordial and always has been. I'm certain her quickness to smile at everyone and be friendly helped her in the jobs she held in her lifetime. This facet of her personality remains strong.

Most times when we visit, she introduces us around. It shouldn't matter that she's already introduced us to every aide there. I wish they would just smile and say, "Nice to meet you," rather than point out they already met us. Mom doesn't remember. What is the point of correcting her over something so small?

April, week 3 (172 weeks)

I had heard many people who are dealing with a relative suffering from dementia talk about how they repeat themselves. They seem to be comfortable reliving a specific period in their life, a year or a decade, and that's what they talk about each visit. Mom has not done that. Mom doesn't recall anything. We don't attempt to force her to remember. Sometimes I will do my own reminiscing and hope she will recall something and add to the conversation, but that never happens. I suppose there's no cookie-cutter dementia sufferer; they're all snowflakes.

April, week 4 (173 weeks)

Mom and I were working on a jigsaw puzzle, and, suddenly, I heard the singing resident from down the hall. This time, she was belting out an unfamiliar tune, a short refrain repeated over and over. She doesn't have a pleasant voice; there's a gravel monotone to her singing with lots of painful flat spots. Soon, another voice joined her in this ditty, apparently trying to drown her out, which caused her to caterwaul even louder. The second voice would eventually yield, and the first would continue with her solo a bit quieter. A few seconds would pass, and the challenge would begin again. This went on for over a half hour. The entire time, Mom was oblivious to the noise. I didn't bring it to her attention. Possibly it was commonplace to her and she had become deaf to it. At that moment, I envied her.

May, week 1 (174 weeks)

Mom likes to show me her jewelry often. If things are in a drawer or closet, they don't exist to her, so we leave the beads, necklaces, and bracelets hanging on the jewelry trees on top of her dresser. We risk the shoppers making off with things, but there is nothing of true value displayed, and most of the aides know where the jewelry belongs; it eventually finds its way back.

Under the jewelry trees are several sectioned plastic boxes with earrings arranged by color. Most of the earrings are costume jewelry clip-ons, but Mom doesn't care. They are shiny and colorful, and she is very proud of her collection. As I admired her treasures with her, I noticed a ring mixed in with the earrings. I picked it out and examined it; it appeared to be a wedding ring. It may have been Mom's or possibly my grandmother's. I didn't ask her because I knew she wouldn't remember. I just palmed it and stuck it in my pocket. I was thankful that this piece hadn't been discovered before by anyone else. It will now belong to my niece, the only girl grandchild.

May, week 2 (175 weeks)

Mom has a standing appointment weekly at the salon on the premises. I like the stylist who is friendly and kind to the women she services. She told me one day that, sometimes, Mom seems anxious, and she will stroke Mom's hand to calm her down. I appreciate the extra care she admonishes on her clients.

The bill for Mom's salon appointments came yesterday. The policy is to have the resident sign for services so that you can be assured they are getting what you pay for. It struck me funny that for all of April, she signed her maiden name. For over seventy years, she has been an Anderson (married at eighteen). What an odd thing to forget.

May, week 3 (176 weeks)

I visited Mom after work today and found Karen also visiting.

I experienced another first; mind you, it was midafternoon, and one of the residents appeared in the dining area in her nightgown, swishing and swirling. I did not want to see what that gown is concealing! I do not want that image etched in my mind for eternity. Mom didn't even appear to notice. I pointed out the woman to my sister, and Karen responded that this woman was really crabby and negative (though she appeared happy and aloof to me). Karen added that she gets annoyed with the aides who help residents when they've misplaced their walkers, yelling at them, "Just let him fall!" Yeah, I guess that qualifies as negative. It's just another day at the home.

May, week 4 (177 weeks)

I tried to share with Mom the details of Pierce and Missy's upcoming wedding. I was afraid she might ask if she was invited, but she didn't. I don't think she understood who Pierce and Missy were. She just smiled a lot as I told her about the bridal shower and the wedding dress. She was happy to let me ramble and feigned interest.

I sure miss my mother. There are so many things I would love to share with her, and it's no longer possible. I feel like I've been grieving the loss of my mother for the past three years. Maybe that's why I've found it so hard to visit her; it's the grief.

May, week 5 (178 weeks)

Mom asked where her purse was. I told her it was in her room, in a drawer. This time, the answer didn't pacify her. Finally, after she asked a couple of more times, I told her I would go get it. I went to her room and brought the purse back with me. She made a big sigh of relief. After about ten minutes, I picked up the purse when she wasn't looking and brought it back to her room, hiding it again in the drawer. She never noticed and didn't ask about the purse again. Rather than to argue with her, I let her have her way, and it calmed her. Again, this is one of the rules that the clinic expert stated repeatedly. It works in a harmless situation like Mom wanting her purse, but I still refuse to allow it to be the rule we live by in every circumstance.

Up to now, my visits have been on weekends or my day off. Sometimes I would take a longer lunch hour and run out to see her. There was the occasional doctor visit that required me to take a half day off of work. I will no longer have to be concerned with those things because I am officially retired. I shared that bit of news with Mom, and she responded, "That's nice." I don't think she remembered that I had a job.

June, week 1 (179 weeks)

The house dog rode up the elevator with me. He has free rein of the building. He exited as the doors opened and headed around the corner to the dining room. It was just after lunch, and he knew there would be lots of treats to be gobbled up under the tables. I swear animals can tell time; he knew exactly when to wait for the elevator.

Mom has never liked large dogs. Every time she would see him, she would comment, "Oh, what a big dog," and then voice her concern that she hoped he wouldn't come near her. She always asked whose dog it was when he came to visit the third floor. One time, I told her it was hers. She did not like that answer. It is better received to say he is just visiting and would be gone soon.

June, week 2 (180 weeks)

When I visited Mom the other day, I sat and watched as she so enthusiastically took part in the sing-along. I didn't want to interrupt because she seemed to really be enjoying the activity. She doesn't have a pleasant singing voice, yet she was the loudest.

I watched the residents, some of whom couldn't stay seated, in their determined confusion. I began to count the number of close calls of injured toes with all the wheelchairs and walkers weaving around. A couple of times, I gasped as the near misses occurred. It was truly amazing how oblivious they all were and how no one got a crushed toe.

The sing-along ended, and the aide pointed out to Mom that I had come to visit. She was thrilled to see me, waving and announcing, "My daughter's here!"

June, week 3 (181 weeks)

This was a happy week for me! Pierce and Missy got married. It was a wonderful weekend of celebrating. The weather cooperated for a beautiful outdoor ceremony. It was so meaningful and just plain fun.

There was also a bit of melancholy for me since Allen was not here to enjoy this occasion. I prepared myself to emotionally handle that fact. I also felt sad that Mom was not there to witness this joyous event. She had been a guest at the other grandsons' weddings, but this time, I had to leave her out. I absolutely understand that bringing her to the wedding would have been a disaster; cruel for her and difficult for me at best, yet I feel sad about the omission. I really miss how life used to be.

June, week 4 (182 weeks)

When I visited Mom on Monday, she was without her glasses again. I mentioned it to an aide, and before long, they were found. I wonder whose face they ripped them off this time.

She is also missing another tooth. Her front teeth had become discolored, and I was concerned that possibly they were dead. I signed Mom up for a dental appointment with the visiting dentist a few months ago and paid a ridiculous fee for the examination even after they indicated that Mom was uncooperative. At this point, I don't believe Mom could tolerate the process of getting dentures or a bridge. She's adjusting to her new appearance of a missing of front tooth, or possibly she thinks she has always looked this way.

I brought some pictures from the wedding to show her. I feared she may wonder why she wasn't in attendance, but she didn't. I had to tell her who each person was. With every picture of the bride, she'd issue an elongated "ooooh," and she'd giggle at every picture of my youngest grandson. The rest of the family didn't get much of a reaction.

July, week 1 (183 weeks)

We will begin looking for another facility. I've crunched the numbers, and I can see an end to the money. I don't regret getting her in this place. We felt like we wanted her to have it as nice as possible for as long as possible. This is a classy joint.

There have been a couple of issues in regard to her care that have caused us concern. On the other hand, I wonder if we'll be satisfied anywhere we go.

Our decision to move her to a companion suite nearly a year ago was partly out of concern that she was frightened at night being alone and partly because of finances. I've felt guilty about that decision the entire time. Mom has never complained; my guilt is due to my observations and my feeling that we may have been manipulated into that decision.

July, week 2 (184 weeks)

It's been a busy Sunday: church, breakfast with friends, two trips to Kendall's Shoe Store (one to buy $200 shoes for Mom by describing her feet, and the second to return the $200 shoes), and visits to Mom's between the shoe store trips.

We got rid of the slippery soled shoes and the clogs. She's down to one pair, and I thought she should have at least two. I may have to wait for a good day and take her to the shoe store. She gets so nervous when she leaves her third-floor refuge; I avoid taking her out if at all possible. To top that off, I'm afraid she might not be agreeable to someone messing with her feet. I don't know if I'm up for it.

Karen reported that the other discolored front tooth was missing. After the loss of the tooth, she looked in a mirror and simply stated, "I don't have many teeth left." She then applied her lipstick and smiled. Her prior vanity has succumbed to the dementia. As long as she seems to accept her new appearance, we will too.

July, week 3 (185 weeks)

I ran out to Chapman House, a memory care facility that has been around for many years. I have heard good things about them. I was apprehensive because I thought they would be far beyond our price range. I was surprised when the sales director shared the price guide. If Mom falls in the level that I think she fits, it's actually several hundred less than what we are paying currently. We must prove we have at least two years' worth of funds to pay her rent before applying for elderly waiver if it's needed. Of course, she must be assessed, and that will determine which level she is placed in.

I'm anxious to share my find with Karen.

July, week 4 (186 weeks)

I set up another tour at Chapman House and brought Karen with me. She was impressed. We liked that it's a one-story building, and each section had a courtyard. Mom could actually go outside (accompanied, of course). In each common area, there was an aviary for residents to enjoy. They also had an activity director who kept the residents engaged pretty much all day.

We had our list of questions, and they were ready with answers that satisfied us. We asked about the ratio of staff to residents, training, and continued education in dealing with dementia. We asked about bathing and toileting. We tied them up for over an hour with our inquest. It turns out that the geriatric doctor who sees Mom currently is also the doctor who services this facility. That will be nice for her. The pharmacy is also the same, so it will be convenient to simply switch the delivery location.

We mentioned that Mom has begun swearing and asked how that would be handled. They were quick to say, "Redirection." Their reaction to this fact was not one of shock. They were actually supportive, commenting that this is something that can occur with dementia and often simply runs a course. Every question we asked was met with a positive answer.

We stopped for lunch after the tour and were excited about the possibility of moving Mom to this location. I'm not sure I even tasted the food; I was too busy talking and planning. I was relieved to find that my napkin had slipped from my lap to the floor; for a moment, I thought I may have eaten it.

July, week 5 (187 weeks)

We had the evaluation for Mom today to move her to Chapman House. Two staffers from Chapman House came out to meet Mom and interview her. They use a point system in their evaluation for placement. Fortunately, most of the points are tallied from her needs (medications, attention, bathing, etc.) and not from her answers to questions. She answered, "I don't know" to "What's the day?" or "What's your mother's maiden name?" or "What's the name of the place you live?" It wasn't as though she was being difficult; she flat out didn't remember. The only question she answered differently was "How old are you?" to which she responded, "I wish I knew!" like it was information we were withholding from her. So the nurse asked, "How old do you think you are?" Mom answered "Sixty. Does that sound right?" Mind you, several times in the process, she had pointed out to the nurse that we were her daughters. So with that answer, I leaned toward the nurse and said, "I'm sixty-four." It wasn't that I actually believed the nurse would buy Mom's answer; I was emphasizing how far off she was. Mom was very surprised that she would soon be ninety.

As part of the assessment, they are reviewing the care notes from Mom's current residence. We should hear in a day or two if they will take Mom and in what level she will be placed.

August, week 1 (188 weeks)

I heard from Chapman House, and they will be accepting Mom as a new resident. She will have her own room in the midstage dementia wing, where I had hoped she would be placed. Of the memory care centers we checked out, this was the only one that grouped residents by their stage of the disease. No longer will she have to be annoyed with people who don't play bingo right!

Our move will happen within the next two weeks. We have a lot to accomplish in fourteen days. This time, we will hire movers. There are companies that specialize in moving the elderly into care facilities. They take pictures of her current surroundings, pack, move, and unpack, setting the room up to look as familiar as possible. After two moves in three years, the entire family is spent. No one has the time, energy, or desire to be involved in another Grandma Louise relocation. I think the expense to hire a moving company will be well worth it.

I'm excited for Mom to move to this new place, to have her own room again. Chapman House is similar with regard to décor. Mom still enjoys an elegant atmosphere, and we are thrilled to provide that for her. There are minor differences between the two care centers; I feel like we're making nearly a lateral move. The major difference is that we won't have to worry when the money runs out. This facility will transition to elderly waiver, so we won't have to worry that Mom will have no place to live or end up in a facility picked by the state.

I don't know when it happened, but I'm feeling much more comfortable with Mom and find I'm not avoiding visits as I used to. She strikes me as so innocent and vulnerable. I no longer feel sad for me; I feel sad for her.

August, week 2 (189 weeks)

I signed the paperwork for Mom's move next week. It was a bit more expensive than I expected, but I still think it's worth it.

Karen and I visited Mom before the representative of the moving company got to Rosewood to give us a quote. We found Mom belting out tunes in the sing-along. She's always disappointed when that activity is over, so we took her downstairs to the bistro for coffee and a cookie to raise her spirits. She rode the elevator like it was the Corkscrew at Valley Fair, whooping it up the two-story descent. She scarfed the cookie and guzzled the coffee. She now takes her coffee with two sugars and cream; something new. I suppose after eighty years of black coffee, it's time to mix it up. If she has a cup in front of her, it has to be full. After three cups, we cut her off (removed the cup from her sight).

We haven't told her she's moving and probably won't until we pull in the lot at Chapman House. She's been at Rosewood for two years and doesn't remember she lives here, so the whole thing may be a nonissue for her.

After our visit with Mom, we stopped by a store looking for something to hang on her walls. Karen found a plaque that we decided against, but it was funny (and appropriate). It read, "Out of my mind . . . back in 5 minutes."

August, week 3 (190 weeks)

This day of moving Mom to the new place was truly remarkable! It was a long day, and I'm exhausted, but that's my only complaint.

We never did tell her that she was moving; we said we were going out to lunch, which wasn't a lie because we had lunch at Chapman House. The drive was close to a half hour, and she didn't say, "Boo." We were concerned that the long ride may cause her to become anxious and had a plan of stopping for ice cream should that occur.

We made it to Chapman House without incident and without ice cream. We had lunch followed by working on a puzzle (it was missing lots of pieces and had extra ones that didn't belong). We got her settled in the activity area for a sing-along and were treated to an ice cream cone before it began.

Then we suggested that we go to her room and brought her there. It was all set up, even pictures on the walls. Her only comment was "Look at all the jewelry." Then she said, "I gotta go pooh." I guess she was *home*.

While Karen finished organizing the closet and drawers, I got Mom set up for bingo with the other residents. That was the only negative of the day. She would angrily yell no when she didn't have the number called. I could hear other residents grumbling and tried to gently correct her. She yelled no after the next number was called and added (very loudly), "You're an asshole!" Oh, boy, I couldn't look at anyone; I was so shocked and embarrassed. I felt like the mother of a misbehaving child on the first day of preschool. I just told her, "Mom, you don't talk like that." She seemed to behave after that, but I wondered how long that would last. I decided to head out while she was occupied. To be honest, I don't think she will last long in this section; her outbursts may land her in the next level. That will be all right, I guess; she should be with people who are similar to her, experiencing dementia at a comparable level.

Overall, today was a success. We just have to take it day by day. Today was way better than expected! I credit the power of prayer.

August, week 4 (191 weeks)

Karen and I are visiting Mom more frequently to assure she adjusts to this new place. Once I'm convinced she is well cared for and content, I will resume weekly visits. I am so thankful to be retired so that I can maintain the current schedule.

I was fairly apprehensive about my visit to see Mom today because she had a very bad Sunday according to Karen. She had visited Mom and found her unable to get up from a chair, unwilling to eat and having trouble speaking. She was very irritable and yelled at people, including Karen.

We were hoping to find her in better shape today, and we did; she was talking and smiling, though she still seemed a bit unstable with walking.

She had an appointment with her doctor this morning at Chapman House. We informed him of her weekend, which we found very disturbing. The facility had called me on Sunday to explain a problem with her medication. Apparently, she had run out of one medication, and the pharmacy sent it to Rosewood, therefore refusing to refill it for the Chapman House. She ended up missing three days of twice daily doses. It's a medication for her restless legs (an antiseizure med), one that should not be abruptly stopped. They figured out the problem, and she would get her evening dose on Sunday. Meanwhile, it threw her into a tailspin. I assume that is why she had trouble walking and speaking when Karen saw her.

The doctor, as expected, didn't want to throw the nursing staff under the bus, but I suspect he felt it was inexcusable too. There are a whole slew of things I'd like to complain about in regard to this episode. I'm giving it a couple of days so that I can regain composure.

We asked the doctor about the possibility of physical therapy because of the change in her gait. He recommended that a therapist come out in a couple of days to work with her.

The nurse who accompanied the doctor looked at Mom's records and commented that the nursing staff of Chapman House had contacted them one evening reporting that Mom was disturbing the other residents by making animal sounds. Now, that's a new one! I was concerned with her swearing; now she's making barnyard noises.

I think I need to give it another couple of weeks before I ask about the next level at this facility. I'm not sure the section that Mom was placed in is the right fit. She needs more than suggestions to join the group in the activity room or visit the restroom. When we spoke with the sales director and nurse before we made our decision, we asked about toileting, since it was our concern that Mom may become dependent on adult diapers if left to her own designs. The answer was that she would be toileted every two hours. I understood that to mean someone would escort her to a restroom, or at least see that she used one. The only thing I have witnessed is the activity director mentioning to the group of twenty residents that, soon, lunch would be served, so "it would be a good time to visit the restroom."

This is not exactly what I was hoping for.

September, week 1 (192 weeks)

I sent an e-mail to the director regarding the medication debacle last week. I recommended they have a better plan B so that a resident isn't without medication for any period. I've heard nothing back.

Mom turns ninety this week. She doesn't know that it's her birthday and doesn't remember how old she is. It's quite a milestone, so Karen and I decided to try to take her out to a restaurant for a celebration lunch with all our kids and grandkids. I'm hoping it will go smoothly with no animal noises or loud hollering, "Coffee, coffee, coffee!" while banging a cup on the table. She is extremely impatient at mealtime. She doesn't converse, so keeping her occupied is the challenge. I thought I might pick up a couple of small jigsaw puzzles from the dollar store and enlist the great-grandsons to assist her in putting them together.

I did her nails on Friday so she'd look nice on her birthday weekend (another one of the promises that they're not making good on—"Oh, yes, we do their nails every week"). After I finished her nails, they definitely didn't look professionally done, but she was happy with them.

I hope we don't stress her too much trying to acknowledge this special birthday. I may have to anticipate a huge tip.

September, week 2 (193 weeks)

Mom's birthday lunch on Sunday went better than I ever imagined! I was concerned because on Friday, when Karen visited her, she couldn't stay awake. She had trouble walking or even talking. You just never know how you will find her. We decided if we found her in the state she was in Friday, we wouldn't try to take her out.

We arrived at Mom's just before eleven and found her asleep in a chair by the aviary, but she woke easily and was happy to see us. We got her up to go to the activity area for a cup of coffee and a cookie. She walked with long strides, not the usual short shuffle. Apparently, the physical therapy is working, even though she fights it, acting annoyed with every instruction.

We told Mom that we were taking her out to lunch, to which she responded, "Goodie, goodie!" We had her visit the restroom, reapply her lipstick, and got her out to the car.

During the ten-to-fifteen-minute drive, she kept reading road signs and pointing out the trees and trucks. Karen and I chuckled at her chatter and commented how nice it was for us to find amusement rather than annoyance.

When we arrived at the restaurant, there was a side salad waiting for Mom, so we bypassed her normal anxiety while waiting to be served. She took turns using the fork and her fingers. After about five minutes of her scraping the plate with her finger to lick the dressing off, I removed the plate. I ordered two meals that I thought she would like and let her pick; I took the other. She had Swedish meatballs. She asked if she was doing good as she finished her mashed potatoes and asked the same after her carrots. She wasn't able to finish all the meatballs. She commented that she couldn't figure out why she wasn't hungry. I took the tally for her of cookies, a salad, and big dinner, stating that she must be full up to the top. I added, "In fact, I think I see mashed potatoes coming out of your nose." She laughed and then said, "I like you."

The fifteen of us sat at a long table with Mom at the head. She didn't seem to wonder or care who was dining with her; she remained focused on the food in front of her. I imagine that most of the family was shocked by her decline over the past year.

When it was time to leave, she loudly repeated, "Here I go!" as she slowly worked her walker through the restaurant. Normally, I avoid the stare of strangers, but this time, I noticed people smiling.

I have a new theory: When she gets tired and is fighting to stay awake, she gets loud. When we got her seated in the car, it took her less than a minute to fall asleep.

September, week 3 (194 weeks)

Well, Mom had quite the week. She finished physical therapy and is scheduled for speech therapy, not because she now lisps with no front teeth but because they want to observe her eat, looking for swallowing issues. In the later stages of dementia, swallowing can be difficult.

We had to run her to the dentist because of yet another loose tooth that bothered her. Getting Mom in and out of the car is a chore. She can't figure out how to do it, so it takes some time, and we worry about her losing her balance. Once in the car, she's somewhat uneasy but busies herself with all the junk in the backseat, randomly handing us receipts and empty packaging.

She ended up having the tooth pulled, so now she's only got the canines and molars on the top and a couple on the bottom. Regardless, she puts on her lipstick and smiles broadly at everyone. I'm surprised how accepting she is of her appearance especially since she always had a streak of vanity. She never passed a mirror or any reflection in a window where she didn't pause to admire herself (she was an extremely attractive woman). Honestly, I'm happy it doesn't bother her and that she's become a roll-with-it kind of gal.

September, week 4 (195 weeks)

Karen shared with me what a great visit she had with Mom the other day, how Mom wanted to walk in the courtyard, and how observant she was. She pointed out plants and lawn ornaments.

I went to see her yesterday just after lunch and found her slumped in a wheelchair at a table in the dining room, sound asleep. I could not wake her. I called her name; I stroked and grasped her hand. I shook her shoulder. I ran my fingers through her hair. I tapped on her arm and knee. I stopped short of throwing a bucket of water on her. I've never seen anyone that sound asleep.

The aide came over and told me Mom had been up all night. She had slept through breakfast but ate half of her lunch. I asked about the wheelchair she was in because Mom uses a walker. She told me that Mom was too tired to walk.

Even though Mom didn't know I was there, I sat with her awhile longer and listened in on a conversation that two women at a nearby table were having. These two were discussing holiday plans. They had to be in their midnineties. The one expected she would go to her parents' farm, and the other asked, "Are they still alive?"

October, week 1 (196 weeks)

I visited Mom today and found her asleep at the dining room table with a fork in her hand. I tried over and over again to wake her. She would only make a grunt and drool.

I met Ida (apparently Mom's new best buddy). Ida and I had a nice visit. Ida seemed to be fairly with it; she repeated herself a few times but was aware of time and place. She was from North Dakota but knew she was in Minnesota. I learned (three times) of her pinched nerve. She has a good heart (she told me). Ida was concerned that Mom couldn't wake and encouraged me to keep trying because Mom wouldn't want to miss the accordion music planned for two o'clock. Each time I tried, she'd barely open her eyes but would drool a lot. Finally, they gathered the group to go for the music and left Mom hunched in her chair. Ida was gone; I had no one to talk to. I took the pile of drool-saturated tissues and tossed them in the trash. Before I left, I kissed Mom on the forehead and said, "I love you, Mom." She responded, "Ay ouv ewe ooo," without even opening an eyelid and went right back to sleep.

I called Karen later to tell her of this troubling visit. Karen shared with me that pretty much every time she visits Mom, Mom is alone. She is never with the group doing an activity. Karen feels Mom is being ostracized.

October, week 2 (197 weeks)

I got the call I was expecting; Mom will probably be moved to the next level at Chapman House. I have mixed feelings; even though I never thought where they placed her to start with was a good fit. Their concern is the "neighborhood" and that they are troubled by Mom's outbursts, which, it turns out, they have been trying to medicate away. In Mom's drug stash, there is one for agitation to be administered "as needed" (this may explain why I find her sound asleep in a chair, unable to wake).

I placed a call to her doctor asking about this medication and its side effects. I'm surprised that no one has bothered to tell us that they are medicating Mom for agitation. Apparently, when the home feels there is an issue, they call the doctor and get permission to administer the medication. I thought back to the time when the doctor's nurse brought up the animal noises; that must have been a call to request the agitation drug. Nobody has told us about this practice.

What we have observed is that Mom's outbursts 90 percent of the time are fairly loud exclamations of success. When she successfully negotiates her butt into a chair, "Woo-hoo!" When she successfully arises from a chair, "Woo-hoo!" Granted, she has vocalizations of disappointment during bingo, but, apparently, the *neighborhood* has become one of bullies who chastise her for all outbursts and refuses her normal courtesies like passing her the bread at mealtime (even though her request has been polite, in normal tone of voice, accompanied by the word "please"). Mom's behavioral issues are a result of the dementia and can't be corrected. I guess I'm disturbed that they are trying to medicate her into compliance for the comfort of others. If she was violent, I might be able to understand it better.

We will go tomorrow to tour the next level. I am in favor of getting her out of the current location, but for her comfort, not the others'. Hopefully, being with people who are more like her will be better. Hopefully, they won't need to medicate her for someone else's sake. I like hearing "woo-hoo." It's a happy noise. Mom's moving on up, woo-hoo!

October, week 3 (198 weeks)

Karen and I met with the head nurse and toured the section they intend to move Mom into; depressing at best, costly at worst. This area is not the *next* level; it's the final level. We noticed about eight residents who are mostly in wheelchairs with a few who stroll aimlessly about. None of them appear conversational. None of them smile. My mind flashed on a movie I had seen, *Night of the Living Dead*. Though the area was bright and nicely decorated, there was a feeling of gloom that hung heavy in the air.

Both of us displayed the usual Anderson girl behavior; we cried. We didn't sob or wail, just the strained voice and welled-up eyes with the occasional tear making its escape down the cheek. Maybe we haven't witnessed the behaviors they contend have occurred, but if in fact they did transpire, were they so terrible to warrant this punishment? Our issue is why weren't we informed? Also, in regard to medicating her for what they deem as unacceptable behavior, her doctor was sought out for authorization, but again we weren't informed. We're dealing with shock along with concern.

Our other irritant is that this particular wing was a huge secret. We asked why we never toured this area prior to move in, since it was a possibility she would be moved there. In the contract we signed, there was a statement that they were allowed to move Mom if they deemed necessary. We have no say in this decision. Any rational person would assume that in a line of progression you expect to go from point B to C, and then D, etc. Mom's progression accelerated from B to F, and we haven't the right to disagree. I feel so naïve that I trusted people to have my mother's best interests in mind.

Mom's behaviors were documented at the last place, and they procured her records for the purpose of assessment. They were aware of her outbursts. I contend they purposely assessed her incorrectly to get us in, and now, two months later, we're forced to pay over a grand more a month. We probably would have continued to shop (though I doubt the perfect or near-perfect senior care facility exists). It's not about the money; we stated several times our main concern is our mother's comfort. I told them we felt like we fell for a sales pitch. I admitted that I didn't think where they placed her was the right fit from pretty much day one, which brings me back to our ignorance of the option.

I could tell the nurse was approaching her wit's end with us. She went to get the paperwork, but the director of sales returned. She heard we weren't happy. She was going to bring our complaints to the management. Sorry, I don't believe it. The bottom line is that Mom will probably be moved tomorrow. I warned them that we will be watch dogs.

We may be back to searching out other facilities. I honestly don't feel we have unrealistic expectations. We asked all the right questions, and they gave all the right answers. The problem is that they know what to say; they just don't implement what they claim.

I decided to quit thinking and analyzing Mom's situation for the rest of the day. Thinking about it doesn't change anything. Instead, I watched my cat Stella abscond with yet another Halloween knickknack. She likes to bring them to the bathroom because they really fly across the floor when she bats at them. It's a pleasant diversion.

To keep myself diverted from my concerns about Mom's situation, I will wrap up all these issues in a nice bundle and hand it all over to God.

October, week 4 (199 weeks)

I called the head nurse at Chapman House and expressed our desire to have better communication. I'm shocked that they don't inform us of Mom's medications but go directly to the doctor for approval. I got a phone message from the doctor's nurse letting me know they were changing Mom's medication and acknowledging that with the move to the new wing, she will not be medicated as she is now. We didn't know they were medicating the "behaviors" out of her in the first place but suspected it. When I would ask why Mom was unresponsive, they would claim she was tired. Never once did they cite the true cause—medication.

The move is scheduled for later today. The new area has fewer residents, so it's a better ratio of aides to residents. I plan to visit tomorrow morning. I will be observant hopefully with an open mind. My resolve continues to be Mom's comfort.

Mom is very social even though she's no longer conversational; she is still a good listener or pretends to be. She loves being in the midst of people. When we visited yesterday, we found her at a large table where they had just finished having a treat with their coffee. The lady next to Mom had only taken a nibble of her cookie, and Mom was offering to buy it from her for a dollar, which she told her she would give her tomorrow. It struck us funny; she doesn't have a dollar, nor would she remember she owed it to someone. She sure wanted that cookie.

After the treat, they had a bean bag competition. They don't seem to make the effort to include Mom, so when we're there, we see that Mom is part of the activity. Mom didn't want to participate, but she enjoyed being the cheering section sitting nearby. She would make sounds of joy when someone managed to toss a bag in the hole and noises of disappointment when they missed. I leaned toward Karen and whispered, "They better rush over and give her a pill. She's making noise." I need to dump that sarcastic cynicism. I vow to be attentive, but I don't want to be anticipating that everything is an attack on my mother. However, as advised by my friends, I will trust my gut.

October, week 5 (200 weeks)

I visited Mom this morning in her new area. I was glad to see that she appeared oblivious to the move. This new wing is vastly different in regard to the residents. Mom didn't seem to notice. She just smiled at us a lot; I think she was happy to see us. She was enjoying the live piano music and commented, "Isn't this nice?" She didn't notice, or didn't mind, the woman removing her pants in the kitchen, the two women in wheelchairs who got in a slapping match and had to be separated, or the woman who fell asleep leaning on Karen.

I told Mom it was Karen's birthday today, and Mom asked her how old she was. Then she asked, "Well, how old am I?" We told her ninety. She responded, "In ten years, I'll be a hundred." She can still do math. Honestly, I don't wish another decade on her, but whatever time she has left, I hope she can keep smiling and say, "Isn't this nice?"

November, week 1 (201 weeks)

Usually, when I arrive in the morning, there's an activity going in the common area that is the hub of the different residential sections. There would be eight to ten residents catching up on current events, tossing a ball around, or playing a game of trivia. Today, the room was empty. I proceeded through the locked door to Mom's area and found her in her room. She smiled when I entered, and I suggested we go find a cup of coffee. It dawned on me that since Mom never remembers where her room is, if I find her there, that means she has been placed there. Karen contends that they are punishing Mom for her outbursts. I certainly hope not.

Mom and I went out to the common area beyond the secure door that has a keypad to gain access. I lucked out, finding cookies to go along with the coffee. I found a newspaper and thought I might find something to read to Mom. Every article was fear, disaster, or shootings. I turned the pages until I came across the obituaries and decided the newspaper thing was a bad idea.

Soon, it was time to set her up for lunch. We went back through the secure door, and I seated her at the table. She promptly grabbed the spoon and began banging it on her empty plate as accompaniment to her hollering, "Bring me something good to eat!" This is one of the things that got her placed in this wing. To me, it seems like there would be a simple solution: don't put an empty plate and silverware in front of her.

I assured her lunch was coming. She expressed she hoped it was yellow. Then she asked me if I liked yellow and would we be having it at my house. I answered yes. The food came, and I cut the meat for her at which point she wanted me to feed her. That was a new twist, but I complied. As she chewed, she made funny faces at me. I just made the faces back at her. She seemed amused. Weird fits so well in that place.

November, week 2 (202 weeks)

Day 1

We are visiting Mom more often since her move to this unit. One or both of us try to see her every day. We have yet to find her participating in an activity. I haven't seen any of the residents from Mom's area involved in the activities.

We almost always find Mom alone, slumped in a chair at the dining room table, asleep. We figure she has been there since breakfast, probably two hours. When we wake her and suggest coffee, she is always eager to do that. If there is an activity, she often wants to participate or at very least observe it. It seems like the only time she gets to do that is when we bring her. We've asked the activity directors why they don't include Mom, and the answer is always that she was asleep. When we find her asleep, we wake her up, and she is always agreeable to do anything we suggest. I wonder if they make the effort. If I had absolutely nothing to do, no one to talk to, nothing to watch or listen to, I'd probably fall asleep too.

Today, they were bouncing a beach ball back and forth in a circle. Mom was eager to join in and made her happy noises, never missing her turn. She even amazed us with some trick shots under the walker.

Even though I can experience a good visit with Mom, I'm not thrilled with this wing. I have several times arrived to find no aides in sight. There are supposed to be three in this section. I can understand if two of them need to assist a resident, but then the third should be watching the others. When the aides *are* around, they don't engage the residents; they talk to each other about their weekend or some such trivial nonsense that should be reserved for break time. There are a few residents that cannot feed themselves, so the aides feed them. While shoveling food into their mouths, the aides don't interact in any fashion with the resident; rather, they talk to each other about their interests. I get the feeling these poor people are simply maintained, not cared for. This place is like a barnyard where the three hired hands are tending the animals.

Day 2 of week 202

Karen called early evening, and I could hear her fighting back tears as her voice cracked. She said, "Mom doesn't belong in that place." She pointed out that Mom has deteriorated quite a bit since the move. Her posture is poor, and it almost appears as though she is unable to lift her head. The decline is obvious, and it has only been three weeks.

We talked about finding her asleep all the time, and when we can get her to wake up, she will drift off to sleep again quite easily. We usually get her up to walk and go out to the area where the activities are. Her walking has become more like shuffling. She is always happy to leave the unit and smiles broadly if there are people in the activity area; she loves being around people. She can't strike up a conversation or even participate other than smiling, but that's still a social response. All she has left is her drive to be social, and we feel she's being denied that. She is isolated and ignored. They are taking the last piece of her personality away.

I have been trying to make the best of a bad situation, but now I realize I have neglected my primary concern—Mom's well-being. I will be calling a couple of the places we toured earlier and another that was on our list but we never got to once we found this place. This is not where we want her to spend the rest of her life.

Day 3 of week 202

The two places that were on our list of possibilities both have waiting lists. Tomorrow, we will visit Willow Brook, the one that we hadn't previously toured.

I took a picture of Mom today after we brought her out to the activity. She was smiling at the people engaged in a current events quiz. Her smile was the only positive thing about her appearance. Her hair was disheveled; clothing wrinkled and mismatched. Her eyes were dark and sunken, shoulders slumped, and it appeared her head was too heavy for her neck to hold it up. Her complexion was grayish. I have never seen her like this.

Whenever we visit Mom, she is so happy to see us and appears in good spirits. Today, Karen was *what's her name.* I'm not sure who I was, but she remembered we always have a good time when we're together.

I wonder if Mom displays the behaviors they complain about when we're not there. We have never witnessed the "animal noises" they claimed she made. I wonder if she's unhappy when she's alone and feels the urge to act out. A child will seek negative attention rather than to accept no attention at all. Maybe that's the same with the elderly.

Day 4 of week 202

We toured Willow Brook and feel no need to look further. Karen and I are so excited and hopeful. We noticed an activity calendar on the bulletin board and saw a group of residents involved in playing a game of ball toss in a circle. A resident was at a table sorting socks, while another was coloring in a book.

This is a new facility, opened in June. As you enter the secure door, you find yourself in the large common area that looks out onto a large porch. The resident rooms are adequately spacious, and all have windows to the outside. The private restrooms have a sink and toilet but no tub or shower; there are bathing rooms down the hall. It's beautiful and functional. The cost has never been our primary concern, but it's nice that we will save nearly $2,000 per month.

We felt the need to explain to the sales director why were seeking a new place so soon after the move to the last one. We couldn't help but do the usual Anderson girl thing—talk through the tears. I showed the director the video I took of Mom slumped in a chair, panning the room to show no aides, just other sleeping or wandering residents. Then I showed her the video I took on Mom's last day at her previous residence when she was involved in a sing-along, only four months earlier. The director commented on the difference in Mom, from vibrant to a lump in such a short time.

We asked how quickly we could get her in and the hope to make this happen within two weeks. An assessment is needed, and they will work to schedule that as soon as possible. We are desperate to get Mom out of Chapman House.

When we left, Karen talked with a couple of ladies having lunch and asked if the food was good (it looked good). They were willing to talk to us and seemed content.

Our plan while we wait is to continue to visit Mom often to keep her occupied and get a little exercise.

Day 5 of week 202

I ran out to visit Mom this morning, and, no surprise, I found her at the dining room table. She was asleep, of course, as were all the other residents. When I woke her, she complained that her legs were bothering her, probably because of sitting for hours in a hard chair. I suggested we walk to unkink her legs. We went to the room where the group was engaged in an activity. We sort of joined in, sitting at a nearby table. She was happy to see all the people, smiling at everyone. Her legs quit aching, and she enjoyed a cup of coffee with me. She was very talkative (mostly nonsense) but kept inserting statements like "You're so pretty" and "We have fun together." We haven't enjoyed anything resembling a conversation in weeks, so even though it made little sense, I was happy with the banter. She really is a trouper. Every day she spends at this place breaks my heart.

Day 6 of week 202

We didn't find Mom asleep in a chair today; we found her asleep on her bed. At least it was a more comfortable spot. It took us some time to get her up. Then we did the giant Barbie doll thing on her. We changed her sweater to one that coordinated better with her outfit, got socks and shoes on her feet, put jewelry on her, brushed her hair, and put lipstick on her. Then we walked her around a bit and had a cup of coffee with her. We got her set up for lunch, and I'm glad we hung around for a few minutes because I stopped them from giving her shrimp (she has a shellfish allergy). It makes me wonder why I filled out all those forms regarding allergies and food preferences.

Day 7 of week 202

When I visited Mom this morning, again finding her asleep at the table, initially, I had difficulty waking her, but she grasped my hand while I sat and watched her sleep. After about ten minutes, she began removing her shirt. She wasn't fully awake. She managed to get one arm out before I could stop her. She wanted the top off, and I explained that she shouldn't because she was in the dining room. She made a couple of more attempts, and I explained a couple of more times the inappropriateness of the action. Finally, she awoke enough to quit trying to disrobe, and she talked a little. We had a nice nonsense conversation. She noticed things around the room and commented on them. She read the room numbers. She pointed out the dark blanket on the white chair. When I joined her in acknowledging the surroundings, she said, "You see that too? That's good because then we know we're both here." She told me I was so good to her, and we had a little "I love you"–"I love you more" argument, which made her laugh. I'm not quite sure whom she thought I was because she mentioned that we were close, even though I was older than her. Like I said, it was pretty much nonsense, but I don't care; it was interaction.

Mom asked how old she was, and I told her ninety. She responded that she wouldn't live much longer. I told her that was all right because she was a Christian and knew where she was going. She responded with a simple, "Yeah." Then another resident joined us at the table. That was out of the ordinary because, normally, Mom is placed at a table all by herself. Mom noticed this woman had a baby (it was a lifelike doll) and told her it was cute. The woman shared that information with the doll.

By now, it was close to eleven thirty and lunch had arrived, so I gave Mom a kiss and told her to be sure to clean her plate.

November, week 3 (203 weeks)

I think the meeting with the nurse from Willow Brook went very well. Linda got to the Chapman House to meet Mom a few minutes before us and found Mom in her room. Mom greeted her with "hello" and quickly added, "I have to go to the bathroom, where is it?" Linda showed her, and Mom proceeded to use the toilet without assistance (and without closing the door). Linda wanted to see how Mom walked, so we all took a short stroll to an area of upholstered chairs by a fireplace. Mom was very cordial and chose to sit on the sofa, giving out a "woo-hoo" when she sat. We pointed out that was an example of the outbursts that landed her in advanced care. Linda asked Mom questions to test her recall. Mom couldn't remember what food is served on Thanksgiving, but when we mentioned turkey, she exclaimed, "I like turkey!" We walked to another area to get coffee, and as soon as Mom sat down, after a "woo-hoo," she patted the table with her palms and demanded coffee. We mentioned patience wasn't her long suit.

Linda asked what we wanted for Mom. I answered that I knew she wasn't going to beat this disease, but we wanted what time she has left to be as pleasant as possible. The entire time, Mom repeated that she has wonderful daughters (I wanted to ask when they would show up but resisted).

By now, it was lunchtime, and I asked if Linda wanted to observe. We brought Mom to her assigned table to dine all by herself (all other tables had two to three people). Linda asked if Mom had any episodes of violent behavior. Absolutely none.

Both Karen and I feel very encouraged. It's not a done deal yet, but I'm optimistic.

November, week 4 (204 weeks)

We were hoping to hear something from Willow Brook, but they must continue the assessment, and reviewing the care notes from Mom's current residence is part of the process. They have experienced difficulty in obtaining the notes. I suppose it was unrealistic for me to expect to have Mom moved so quickly, especially with a holiday in the mix. Getting into December means we will be stuck paying for two places for one month. Again, the money isn't the big issue; getting Mom out of there as quickly as possible is the priority. We want what's best for Mom; I know that it's not Chapman House.

We continue to take turns and visit her daily. The visits are cookie cutter; she is alone, asleep at a table, or sometimes in her room. Once per week, we go together to visit. When we visited today, we found her asleep in a chair in her room. I think they got wise to the fact we didn't like finding her asleep at the breakfast table two to three hours after breakfast. Their excuse for her not being in the activity was, as usual, "she was sleeping." Then why don't you wake her and tell her it's time for a cookie?

I just hope she can hang in there for a little more time until we can orchestrate her escape.

December, week 1 (205 weeks)

Venting! Why is it that people who are hired to work with dementia patients have no understanding of the disease? They don't seem to even have common sense. You would think, at the very least, before reporting for work at a memory care facility, they might read about the condition.

Mom used to be obsessed with her purse. As the dementia has progressed, she's forgotten about her purse; but once in a while, she'll get nervous that she doesn't have it, and we just tell her it's in her room. Normally, she's fine with that. Yesterday, when Karen was getting Mom set up for lunch, one of the aides said, "Louise, where's your purse?" Really? My sister responded with "Just drop it!" Reminding Mom of her purse only creates anxiety in her; that act verges on just plain mean. I could excuse it as innocent ignorance, except for the fact that it was one of the things I asked before deciding to move her there—"Do you have ongoing training for handling dementia?" "Ongoing?" They don't appear to have even preliminary training and are devoid of the slightest understanding. I've witnessed threats and shaming of the residents, including Mom. Maybe it won't be any different anywhere else, and that's a real shame. But if that's true, I'd just as soon save over two grand a month to tolerate it.

Linda from Willow Brook corrected our belief; what we were told was "advanced care" at Chapman House is, in reality, a behavioral unit. We assumed "advanced care" meant they would be giving more attention to Mom because she needed it. Apparently, their idea of advanced care was all about controlling and imprisoning those who need attention.

Willow Brook is suggesting a trial run. They weren't able to procure the care notes from Chapman House because they don't exist for November. That in itself is disturbing. From what Willow Brook did get, notes through October, they seem to be concerned that Mom's behaviors may not fit in their community. My paranoia may be kicking in, or I'm realizing we've all been manipulated. Detailed notes were maintained for a few months including calls to the doctor to request anxiety medication and embellished reports of disruptive behavior such as imitating farm animals. This was proof positive documentation that Mom was uncontrollable, necessitating the move to what Karen refers to as "the Green Mile." Anyone reading these notes would be hesitant to accept Mom as a tenant. Once she was moved where they wanted her in the first place, the notes were no longer necessary. They had done their job well, making Mom out to be an undesirable. Fortunately, I believe Linda also sees the oddity in the lack of care notes since the move into the behavioral unit and the reluctance to share information.

The thought crossed my mind—what if Karen and I are wrong? What if we are in denial? We've been there before. Obviously, we are going to be much more tolerant of Mom's behavior; she's our mother. We could put her through a traumatic shift that may be temporary, or possibly it wouldn't be traumatic because she doesn't seem to know where she is on any given day. She might fail the test and wind up back at square one. There are so many what-ifs. As unhappy as we are with the current situation, I think we need to agree to the one-week trial.

December, week 2 (206 weeks)

Yesterday, Karen found Mom in bed midmorning. The aide said she was tired. Karen woke her and suggested they get a cup of coffee. Karen told Mom that she saw some cookies. At the mention of cookies, Mom practically bolted out of bed. I guess she wasn't that tired.

We decided to go for the trial stay at Willow Brook. Linda must contact Mom's doctor for orders first, and then a date will be picked. My brother-in-law, Gary, made a good point: while they're testing her, we're testing them. We decided we won't know anything unless we try. Mom is going to be Mom, and we can only pray that will be acceptable. All we want is for her end days (weeks, months, years) to be pleasant for her.

I have placed three calls to three different people at Chapman House, the last one with the director. I wanted to inform them of our plan to take Mom away for a week. No one has returned my call. Well, their efforts to hold Mom hostage are about to be thwarted. We are proceeding with the move tomorrow morning. Our major concern in regard to the move is getting her medications. Since no one will return my calls, I've developed a contingency plan. I've shared this apprehension with Linda, and she is willing to assist us in this quest. If we are denied Mom's medications, we will contact the pharmacy and order what she needs, paying for anything that may not be covered by insurance.

Our plan is to get Mom to Willow Brook in time for lunch. While she's eating, we'll get her stuff put away in her room. I hope and pray she passes this audition. I do not want to bring her back to Chapman House!

God made us social animals, and Mom needs interaction; she loves being around people, just grinning at everyone. She still appreciates her presentation; she enjoys wearing nice clothes, having jewelry on, and wearing bright lipstick—even though she's missing her front teeth. They have had her at Chapman House long enough to know what makes her happy. To me, that is part of her care. Put some beads on her, set her in a group of people, give her a cookie, and you've got one happy lady (just don't play bingo).

I am hopeful for this trial to become permanent. Mom needs it; we need it.

December, week 3 (207 weeks)

On the day of the move for the trial run, I picked up Karen at just after eight o'clock to go get Mom packed for her adventure. We found her at the dining room table, asleep. She was very difficult to wake, and we were a bit concerned how we were going to get her out to the car. While she slept, we packed my car with anything we thought she might need and a few items that might be familiar; some angels, photos, clock, and, of course, her racks of beads and bracelets.

Mom was extremely groggy, but we got her out to the car and buckled in. She stayed awake for the car ride pointing out things like the gloomy sky, a stop sign, a big truck. We arrived just before lunch, and they were kicking a ball around in a circle of residents sitting in chairs. Mom joined right in and did very well. I was busy with paperwork while they got her set up for lunch at a table with two others. She fell asleep during lunch.

Karen and I ran out for lunch and returned to put the rest of her stuff away in the room. We found her asleep in a comfy recliner, but she woke when we approached her. She never asked where she was. She didn't appear anxious or confused. She even told Karen, "This is a good day." It made me wonder if somewhere deep in her mind, she understood what was happening.

Linda went over details of the stay with us. She shared what the nurses at Chapman House had told her, and these "behaviors" were noted for observation on her chart at Willow Brook. After each behavior were instructions for how to respond if they occurred. Some of the notations were news to us. "When she's in a mood, she exit-seeks." I disagreed with that.

She was content to be in a secure area. I think she tried doors looking for a bathroom when she had a bladder infection. Another notation was "She makes animal noises such as rooster, duck, and cow." I still can't get my head around that one. We've never heard any of these. I know of no animal that goes, "Woo-hoo."

Linda explained that if her behaviors upset other residents and they react in a negative manner, it upsets the community. It's like the geriatric version of mob mentality. So our hope is that she will be content enough to not act out—no quacking, mooing, or cock-a-doodle-dooing!

Again, Karen and I are taking turns making short daily visits. I went to visit yesterday, and Karen will visit this morning.

Yesterday, Mom was asleep but easy to wake. She told me I was so pretty; then I found her glasses and asked her how I looked now. She wanted to know how old she was and couldn't believe the answer adding, "I don't have much time left." I responded, "Yeah, but just think where you're going," to which she asked, "Where am I going?" I decided to change the direction of our conversation at that point. I asked her how she liked it there. She very emphatically answered that she really liked it a lot. We took a walk down a hall and found a puzzle for us to put together. She understood the concept and was pleased with herself each time a piece fit. Then an aide came to fetch her for lunch. She asked me why Mom was there for a respite stay. I told her that Mom's current residence claims she has behavior issues. The aide responded that she hadn't noticed any. That's encouraging.

Mom sat at the table and greeted the other ladies. I was standing to her left. She turned to her right and addressed the aide fairly loudly, "Where's my daughter?" I told her that I was on her left, and she laughed when she turned her head and saw me. Hopefully, that wasn't considered an outburst. It didn't seem to upset anyone. I left her with the promise to come visit again soon.

Karen called after she visited Mom this morning. She said Mom was like a different person. Mom has had difficulty settling in on words to express herself. Karen couldn't figure out what Mom was trying to say and admitted to her that she didn't understand, to which Mom replied, "Me neither." She's just too funny.

There's no way for us to know how she is doing when it comes to things like dressing in the morning or getting ready for bed or bath time. We can only hope it's not beyond their scope of understanding. They do seem to have more of a grasp on dementia. Mom just seems so much more at ease. Even her posture is much improved.

I'll run out to see her tomorrow. I hope and pray they will decide to keep her. I've got my church prayer network on task too.

December, week 4
(208 weeks—four years)

Merry Christmas! What a wonderful gift we received!

Both of us went to see Mom this morning, hoping to hear a verdict. Karen got Mom involved in the activity, and Linda called me into her office. She said all the staff just loves Mom, and she saw no reason to make her leave. She admitted that Mom displayed one behavior yesterday at bingo; she swore when she didn't get a number, calling the caller an asshole. They removed her from the activity and set her up with coloring a Christmas picture. They understand dementia; redirect. You can't change the patient; you need to change the trigger to the behavior. Mom is so improved just in this one week. She isn't hunched over and walks better with less shuffling. She loves having people to dine with; two Glorias. Having the same name should be easy for anyone to remember, but not Mom. She greets them and gives them a broad toothless grin and often asks their names.

I can't express how relieved and happy we are!

Karen and I ran out to Chapman House to pick up the rest of Mom's pills and more clothes. Of course, the staff (once we found some) wasn't aware we were coming for the medications even though I had called two days ago. Fortunately for them, they did gather what remained and gave to me. One asked if Mom was coming back, and I simply answered no. I felt no need for explanation. We were so happy to leave that place knowing it was the last time we'd ever have to go there.

January, week 1 (209 weeks)

I signed the paperwork last week for Mom's new home. When I arrived, I found her coloring with an aide. Apparently, that's her new interest. She was alert and happy.

The improvement we've seen in her is nothing short of a miracle. She asked the aide what she had on her eyebrow (a piercing). A week ago, she wouldn't have been that observant. She walks around and will stop at a resident who's awake to say hello and ask how they are doing.

Today, we got Mom's stuff all moved over from the old place. We hired the same mover we used last time, and they gave us a deal, since it had only been a few months. They did all the work; hung all the pictures and shelves and displayed all her knickknacks. Apparently, Mom didn't recognize her room because they found her asleep in another resident's bed. She was particularly confused today. She talked a lot of nonsense and couldn't sit still. She was trying doors (what Chapman House called exit-seeking), but when she was directed to a bathroom, she was contented. Our conclusion is a bladder infection. They don't know Mom well enough yet to be aware of odd behavior, so we alerted the nurse to collect a urine sample for testing. A couple of days on an antibiotic should have her back to normal.

We honestly thought a couple of weeks ago she was near the end. The day we packed her things in my car for the trial week, Karen said to me, "I just don't want her to die here." That trial was a long week wondering if they were right about Mom, and we were wrong, in denial. Well, we were right! Any of her behaviors were due to either physical or emotional pains. She doesn't have her memories; the only thing she has left is her social attitude, her personality. They were stripping her of that. She sat alone to eat, was put in her room to sleep in a chair, and was not included in activities. We didn't get her out of there a moment too soon. She was dying. Now she's living and enjoying it. I don't know how much time she has left, but it's going to be quality time.

January, week 2 (210 weeks)

We talked with one of the aides who normally works the night shift. She said Mom gets up often during the night, but she will just take her for a walk and then get her back to bed. They seem so accommodating and patient at this facility. I believe that is partially due to hiring people who aren't there just for a paycheck. We are very pleased.

January, week 3 (211 weeks)

Karen called with a report on Mom. Karen found her asleep, and they had some difficulty waking her, but they got her to the lunch table. She was drowsy but ate and then perked up when they brought her a bowl of strawberry ice cream. That made me remember all the mother-daughter banquets we attended when we were young. The dessert was always Neapolitan ice cream. We would cut it apart; Karen got all the strawberry, I got all the chocolate, and Mom got the vanilla. If there had been a third daughter, Mom would have probably given her the vanilla, and she would have gotten nothing.

After lunch, Karen got Mom walking. They had a tag-along. Robert, a resident who cannot speak, shadowed them down one hall and up another. Leave it to Mom, no matter where she is, no matter what her age, she attracts men. Mom attempted to engage him, saying hello and asking if he knew her. Later, Karen told Mom that Robert couldn't speak, but Mom won't be able to remember that.

January, week 4 (212 weeks)

We went to visit Mom and found her sitting with one of the Glorias, wide awake. I pulled out the puzzles that I bought for the home, and Mom put all three together, with a little help. They were small puzzles, a dozen pieces each, but still provided a challenge for her.

One aide told me that Robert really likes Mom, and she saw them holding hands yesterday. She giggled and said she thought it was so cute.

January, week 5 (213 weeks)

When I went to see Mom this week, she was sound asleep in a recliner. She was dressed and had her jewelry on. Her necklace was an old one with a gold clock dangling in the center. Well, it was meant to dangle, but it was stuck firmly to her blouse by a piece of food from breakfast (something with syrup). Neither I nor the aide could wake Mom fully. She would just barely open her eyes and mumble a word. The aide said she was up all night and crashed after breakfast. I only hope she wasn't disruptive during the night. They were going to let her sleep through lunch but would keep a plate for her in case she woke. She was quite different from my last visit. It's day by day.

February, week 1 (214 weeks)

We went to Mom's today to meet with the new doctor. We were there over two hours by the time we met with the doctor's assistant. We were getting cranky—needed a Snickers. We were hoping to get Mom off of some of the meds they've prescribed for "behaviors." Instead, they're reducing her Tylenol. Big deal. My feeling is these drugs don't make life better for Mom; they make work easier for the staff. Maybe I'm wrong. I will be reading up on these drugs again and be better armed for next time we meet.

The assistant was testing Mom's memory and asked such things as what city is this, what state? "I don't know. I don't know." Then she asked Mom if she knew who we were. Mom hollered over to us, "Who are you?" We chuckled and told her we were her daughters, to which she agreed. The assistant asked Mom what our names were, and Mom hollered over to Karen, "What's your name?" She didn't have even one answer to any of the questions. Oh, well, maybe another day she'll remember our names. At least she can still problem-solve; she knew where to go to get the answers.

February, week 2 (215 weeks)

When Karen and I visited Mom this week, she was awake but uninvolved. She was happy to see us but didn't know who we were.

I gave her a cookie, so I became her immediate best friend. I did her nails (I don't even want to consider what it was that I cleaned out from under her fingernails). I put a magazine under her hands to keep from messing up the table. It was open to some pasta recipes, and Mom was in a reading mood and would read the titles, except she pronounced pasta with a long "*a.*" Paste-a. I didn't correct her. The manicure was a fairly long process, so she read the titles over and over: paste-a recipes, yummy paste-a, summer paste-a, light paste-a. I decided against a second coat of polish. Sometimes these visits can test your patience. What helps is that she's so happy when you're doing something one on one with her.

February, week 3 (216 weeks)

Mom has trouble sleeping at night and always has. We're told she gets up several times during the night. Often, they will take her on a short walk and then get her back to her bed. This week, she added a new twist to her routine—nudity! We had no response other than to giggle a little. On our way out, we ran into one of the aides from the night shift who went into a bit more detail. It turns out they've been putting pajamas on Mom. I don't know whose pajamas, since Mom doesn't own any. She has always slept in a nightgown and has no less than six of them. We figure that Mom thinks she's dressed and disrobes to get ready for bed. She doesn't see a nightgown (hidden behind a closet door), so she heads out for help. Hopefully, when they put her in the correct sleepwear, she'll stay clothed. A ninety-year-old naked woman—that's what nightmares are made of.

Every once in a while, I need to look at the picture I took of Mom at Chapman House so that I can be thankful for our resolve to move her out of there. She is thriving at Willow Brook. The difference is astounding. Today, when we visited, she was involved in exercise. They never leave their chairs; they just move their arms and legs to music, but she followed along doing very well. When it was over, she commented that she had never been to a church like this before.

I went today to see Mom, this time with Karen, mainly so we could do lunch after the visit. We found Mom involved in the activity, which was sitting in a chair and kicking a beach ball if it came near you. Roger had trouble keeping the ball on the floor and would bat it hard. Mom began name-calling. With a very angry face and tone of voice, she'd yell, "Dummy!" The next time, she yelled, "You're stupid!" It must be ninety years of pent-up rage showing through; all those years of a cordial demeanor are just too difficult to maintain. I would tap her on the shoulder and say, "Be nice." She'd just smile at me, and a moment later, she's yelling, "Dummy!" My mother doesn't play well with others.

February, week 4 (217 weeks)

Though I have never heard any of the animal noises that the old place claimed she made, I think I have a new one for their list: chimpanzee. She takes turns between monkey sounds and cackling like a witch. We can't figure out why she likes to make noise. Fortunately, this place doesn't react, and the other residents seem to ignore it.

They even let her play bingo. Losing at bingo is her trigger for swearing. The game is an abbreviated style where they only have five numbers on their card and play until everyone wins. The prize is candy. Mom loves her sweets!

Mom is happy to see us when we visit, though she doesn't remember our names or often what relationship we have with her, but seeing her involved and happy makes us happy. Yesterday, they were playing a game with a beach ball, and Mom was very intent with the process. Apparently, Roger was playing correctly, so Mom didn't have to yell at him. It's so great to see her be a part of the group.

March, week 1 (218 weeks)

Karen visited Mom yesterday. She told me the activity was a game of charades. My first thought was it sounded ridiculously impossible for memory care residents, right up there with Trivia, which they attempted at the last place. Such activities almost seem mean. But Karen said Mom was absorbed in the activity, actually acting out a couple of words, and her actions made sense. The second word she said out loud as she was acting it, so she somewhat missed the point of the exercise.

When I ran out to see her today, I found that they had let her sleep in, so she was just getting moving about at ten thirty. She missed the activity, but she was very alert as she ate some toast and bacon they had made for her.

After she ate, we put a small puzzle together. She made gleeful noises with each piece she slid into place, exclaiming often, "This is fun!" She seems so happy. This place was a very good choice.

March, week 2 (219 weeks)

As I sat with Mom at the table waiting for lunch, she asked to go to the bathroom. The aide reminded her she had just gone but then leaned in closer to her and whispered, "Do you have to go number two?" to which Mom replied, "What's that?" In the hesitation of trying to come up with a different term, I suggested "oopy-doop." I explained that Mom had made up words for all bodily functions; she felt pee, poop, and fart were much too crass. In fact, as kids we thought fart was the F-word. So the aide asked her if she needed to *oopy-doop*. Mom didn't answer, but when the aide asked again if she wanted to use the restroom, she nodded.

When they returned to the table, the silverware had been set at each place. Mom noticed that the other two places at the table had their three utensils in the same order, but hers was in a different order. I told her she could fix hers to match, which she proceeded to do. She named each piece as she moved it, but she didn't say "spoon," "fork," or "knife." She used words I had never heard before, and I don't think they were Swedish. She actually repeated the words once the pieces were in the proper order. I guess she's making up replacement words again. That will make it even tougher to communicate!

March, week 3 (220 weeks)

A few days ago I thought that I'd go to visit Mom early afternoon, since lately, when we visit in the morning, she's not up yet. I got there at about one o'clock and found her napping, sound asleep; so much for that plan. I watched her sleep for about a half hour. It didn't make sense to me to wake her because often I'm a stranger to her these days; why confuse her? I'm still glad I went because it will keep the staff on their toes, knowing someone cares about her. Maybe I should visit after midnight when I know she'll be up.

Today, Karen and I found Mom up and dressed, snoozing in a recliner in the middle of the morning activity. She perked up when she saw us. She seemed a little confused, wondering where she was and if she would be spending the night. She was shocked to learn she lived there and thought the place was too big. We told her she had her own room, which was smaller, and asked if she'd like to see it. We got her up and put her walker in front of her. She pointed at the walker that was parked next to hers and asked Karen, "Is that yours?" I tried to stifle a laugh and let out a snort instead.

March, week 4 (221 weeks)

I arrived at the home late morning today to find Mom awake and attentive. She was all decked out in blue with appropriate beads and bracelets. She had bright pink lipstick on and smiled really big when she saw me.

The visit was going so well, I decided to stay for lunch. Sam, the cook, had invited me to stay several times. He's a very good cook, so I didn't hesitate to accept this invite. Today's lunch included peas, a vegetable Mom used to force me to eat. I still don't like them! Mom apparently loves them. She was focused on the peas, but the fork created a challenge for her. For every five peas on the fork, only two made it to her mouth. The other three rolled off and landed either on her lap or the floor. I suggested she use her spoon, but she ignored me. When no one was looking, I scooped my peas onto her plate. Sam walked by and noticed her devouring the peas and went back to the kitchen, returning with a bowl of peas just for her. She ate all of them (well, those that didn't fall off her fork).

After lunch, I waded through the peas to give her a kiss and say good-bye. She said, "I love you," and yelled "Bye-bye," until I exited the building. These are the visits I live for (except for the peas).

April, week 1 (222 weeks)

Mom and I went for a walk around the hall, and then she announced she wanted coffee. We had picked up a tail to our little parade, a petite woman wearing her coat and pulling a small suitcase. She expressed her desire for coffee too. We walked to the dining area, and they both got seated for lunch.

Mom still makes her noises, and it annoys some of the residents, but the staff just takes it in stride. They are not animal noises, just groans and nonsense words. I mentioned to her that she was loud today, just an observation, not a scolding, and she responded, "That's what I know how to do." I guess she sees it as a talent.

April, week 2 (223 weeks)

Today, Mom asked me twice who I was. The second time I told her, she asked, "Are you sure?"

She was sharing the love freely, telling us over and over again that she loved us. While I was doing her nails, she told me I was a pretty child and asked if I had a boyfriend, to which I responded, "As a matter of fact, no." She acted very shocked and said, "Really? 'Cause you're so pretty." I guess I know where to go when I need an ego boost.

April, week 3 (224 weeks)

Mom was in good spirits yesterday. She doesn't always remember our names, and today she didn't recall how we're connected to her, but somewhere in the recesses of her mind, she knows we've had good times together. Several times she announced, "We have fun together."

They were playing a game of Pokeno (bingo with playing cards) that we got her involved in, risking her swearing, but the worst she came up with was "Gall darn you." Whew! She got a bingo, but they had run out of candy for prizes. Luckily, I had a snack package of Oreos in my purse, so that was her award. I opened it and gave her a cookie. She wanted to separate the Oreo, so I helped her. Before I knew it, she used the two cookie parts as markers on her card. She's resourceful.

April, week 4 (225 weeks)

I found Mom wandering about the main area. She was happy to see me and asked right away where she was going. We haven't gone anywhere since the car ride to this place nearly five months ago. I felt I was disappointing her not to be taking her on an outing. I shifted gears quickly and offered to do her nails. She liked the idea and offered to watch my purse while I got the nail supplies.

I lined up the different bottles of polish, and she picked out a bold pink color. She was very pleased with the outcome. I have to admit, I'm getting pretty good at this job.

We still had a little time before lunch, so I showed her the songbook that went along with a DVD I bought to donate to the care center. It was full of old-time songs in large print. She read a few of them out loud. I think the entire group will enjoy sing-along time.

I put the book away, and I got Mom a glass of cranberry juice. She stuck her finger in it and sucked the juice off. She did that over and over, even after I suggested she drink it. I even showed her by example. Finally, I told her to pick up the glass and drink. She did. I guess I needed to be more specific with my instructions. Lunch was finger food, so I couldn't witness her understanding of the concept of silverware, which she seemed to have trouble with last week. She often asks, "What do I do?" I am wondering if she's forgetting how to eat. I must resist quoting *A Christmas Story*, "How do the piggies eat?"

April, week 5 (226 weeks)

I found Mom enjoying a piece of toast and some bacon when I arrived at the home at about ten thirty; she apparently slept through breakfast. The aide brought her coffee and a couple of creamers. She was drinking the coffee black but kept asking what the little containers of creamer were. She asked about every four seconds, and each time I answered and then asked if she wanted some in her coffee. She didn't, but a few seconds later, we'd go through the banter again. It was good substitute for conversation until it got annoying, so I removed the subject matter from the table.

We joined the activity, which was morning exercises. She did fairly well watching the aide and following the motions. She must have worked up an appetite because she was ready for lunch at eleven thirty. I joined her today. She dripped sauce from the beans on her lap with every spoonful, so I showed her how to scrape the bottom of the spoon on the edge of the bowl. Remarkably, she grasped the idea and ate all of her beans without another drip. Last week, she seemed to have forgotten the purpose of silverware, and this week, she retained an action for several minutes. I think she was having a good day.

May, week 1 (227 weeks)

Mom was thoroughly enjoying the exercise time today. Performed from a seated position, the routine must burn all of fifteen calories. I don't think it would matter to her what they were doing as long as she could be in the group.

I haven't heard her normal voice in weeks. She has decided to speak in a very high-pitched tone. Her favorite word is "hello," which she will repeat over and over to everyone she sees. You must respond with "hello," or her greeting will continue like a never-ending echo.

While we waited for lunch, I touched up her nails but learned a lesson: have her use the restroom first. She refused to visit the restroom before lunch because she didn't want to risk messing up her nails. She doesn't remember how to flip a switch or that you use a spoon to eat ice cream, but she remembers you need to let your polish dry. Go figure.

May, week 2 (228 weeks)

Karen and I visited Mom together today. She was asleep at a table with three other ladies (they were awake). She was easy to wake and happy to see us. Karen noticed she had an odd bump under her shirt and assumed she was having an issue with her bra again; sometimes, it gets twisted. We walked to her room to check it out. We thought one or both of the twins may have been out of their cradles. Not so this time; we found a sock that must have clung to the bra in the laundry. I told Mom she didn't need to pad her bra; she was big enough. We were surprised at how hard she laughed, and it made us laugh harder.

We took a little walk down the hall, taking the long way to get to the dining area, and she said, "I sure am lucky to have good friends like you."

May, week 3 (229 weeks)

A couple of weeks ago, we were surprised to be reunited with an old family friend. As the residents were getting ready to have lunch, Karen noticed a familiar face and asked, "Are you Thelma?" It was. We had known Thelma all our lives; she even lived next door to us for a few years when we were kids. She was a new resident at the home. We were excited and said to Mom, "Look, it's Thelma!" Mom didn't react other than to say her normal "hello" and smile. We could tell that she had no recollection of Thelma, but Thelma remembered Mom. Thelma's daughters came from down the hall, and we shared enthusiastic hugs all around. We explained Mom's condition, and they were saddened to hear it. We know that Mom will have even more advocates with Thelma's family visiting often.

Last time we visited Mom, Thelma told us that one night, she awoke well after midnight to find Mom standing in her doorway. Her room is three doors down from Mom's. That had to feel scary; wake up in the dark and see a figure in your room, just standing there, like something out of a horror movie. Thelma asked her if she needed to use the bathroom. Mom said yes, and Thelma told her to go ahead. She then called the nurse to come get Mom and watched to be sure they got her back to her own room. I'm thankful for Thelma; she wasn't annoyed or even slightly disturbed.

I heard they found Mom asleep in someone else's bed one day. Poor confused Mom.

May, week 4 (230 weeks)

I went to see Mom this morning and found her asleep in a chair. It took some effort to rouse her, but I finally got her to move to a table so I could do her nails. She woke up for a couple of minutes when I offered her a cookie. As I worked on her nails, she fell asleep again. When I was done, she woke up and told me she liked me. She asked if I was cold. I told her it was cool in the building, but outside, it was getting hot. I mentioned it would be a good day to stay inside and take a nap. She responded, "They say people who do that are healthy." I told her she must be really healthy. I was a little shocked; this was the closest to a conversation that we've had in a long time. Then she said, "We sure have fun when we're together." What a turn around. When I got there, I wondered if she might be nearing the end because she sleeps so much. When I left, Mom was like she was two years ago.

June, week 1 (231 weeks)

I brought a bill from the pharmacy with me to the home to ask some questions. It appears they order odd amounts of her meds, and I was concerned that we are billed the co-pay each time. I met Steve, the new nurse, and I introduced myself as Louise Anderson's daughter. He responded, "Hello, hello, hello, hello." I said hello back (only once), thinking he seemed a bit too excited to meet me. Then he added, "She's the one who says hello to everyone?" OK, now I got it! I confirmed that was my mother. He said she's very pleasant and he likes her. She calls him Froggy. I have no idea where that comes from. He's a very nice-looking man, not frog-like at all. I wonder if somewhere in the recesses of her mind she's recalling a classmate or neighbor kid they called Froggy. We'll never know. He doesn't appear to be offended, so that's good. Froggy did make a copy of the bill and promised to follow up on it.

I checked out the medications that Mom is on and learned that they are common for dementia patients, easing their anxiety. The medication for agitation is still on her med list, but it is *as needed*. I don't believe they've given her a dose since she's been at Willow Brook.

She's been here for over six months now. We enjoy the peace of mind we feel. There is no such thing as the perfect senior care facility, but when the issues are fairly minor, it makes it better than tolerable.

June, week 2 (232 weeks)

Mom was having a good today. As soon as I walked in, she waved, and when I approached her, she said, "I love you." However, this visit, she didn't seem to know who Karen was. I guess we take turns in the area of recognition.

Karen showed me a new trick that Mom can do. Karen shuffles a deck of cards and hands a few at a time to Mom, who sorts them, aces to kings. It's not exactly an amazing card trick, but Mom seems to like performing it.

Thelma and her daughter mentioned Mom has made a couple of wee-hour visits again. Karen joked that they may have to get a restraining order taken out on Mom. They laughed.

June, week 3 (233 weeks)

Today, Mom was confused. There was no spark of recognition at all. She seemed to be anxious about something but couldn't explain it. She was looking for something green, and it was important. Finally, I told her she was done with it and someone picked it up. She seemed satisfied with that. To distract her further, I suggested doing her nails. I asked what color she wanted, and she said, "Gray." That must have been to match her mood.

Mom sleeps a lot. I assume she dreams. I wonder sometimes if she has dreamed something and upon waking doesn't realize it was a dream. To her, it's reality. I wonder if she was dreaming about work, maybe a green folder that was important in the dream story. Possibly when Mom is talking nonsense, she's been dreaming.

When we set Mom up for lunch, she wanted to know where the liquor was. Now that sounded like a good idea.

June, week 4 (234 weeks)

Last week, Mom didn't recognize either of us. This week, I'm not sure. She was aware this visit but in a foul mood. They were doing an activity with a ball on a large fabric circle with handles. The ball rolled off the edge, and Mom yelled, "Goddamn, people!" Games are not fun for her; they're serious business.

After the activity, we urged her to take a walk before lunch. She went under protest and maintained a knit brow the entire stroll. When Karen tried to help her use the restroom, Mom swore at her. When we got her set up for lunch, I began to cut the cheeseburger into small bite-sized pieces, since without front teeth, Mom cannot bite a sandwich. I commented that the bun was hard to cut through, and Mom loudly added, "That's ridiculous!" She was downright ornery. I suppose everyone has an off day once in a while; maybe after a nap, she'll awake in a better mood.

Over a burger at a nearby restaurant, Karen and I talked about Mom. Her foul mood wasn't contagious. We enjoyed each other's company while sharing how we felt about the situation. Both of us realized that we no longer feel resentment and are seldom annoyed with Mom. We weren't even troubled by her foul mood today. It feels good to be amused by her actions rather than irritated. She is, in essence, helpless and innocent. We view our role now is to protect her and assure she is well cared for.

July, week 1 (235 weeks)

Entering Willow Brook, you are often met by the drone of Sylvia, "Help, I need help." Truth be told, Sylvia seldom needs help, but she alerts the staff to any issues of other residents. If Barbara is attempting to arise from her wheelchair, Sylvia is the alarm. If Orville is messing with the decorations, Sylvia is quick to rat him out.

Mom was really happy to see me today, and I could see the spark of recognition. Then she said to the fellow next to her, "She's a nice lady." I realized that she comprehended we had a relationship, just not exactly how. She used to tell everyone that we were wonderful daughters; now she's surprised to hear she's a mother. Regardless, she was pretty happy today and didn't swear once while I was there.

July, week 2 (236 weeks)

Though Mom had a momentary lapse in potty mouth, it was short-lived, and she has been swearing a lot lately. She could simply be walking down the hall, and she would curse unprovoked.

Later in the week, the nurse called and informed me that Mom has experienced a decline and suggested we meet with hospice. Hearing the word "hospice" is similar to hearing the word "cancer." I set up an appointment with them for the next day.

The decline seems quite rapid, so our concern is a possible urinary tract infection and not necessarily the progression of the disease. When we talked with the hospice representatives, we expressed this concern. It was decided to rule out a bladder infection before signing her up for hospice.

July, week 3 (237 weeks)

Before any test results were available through Willow Brook, Mom took a turn, and they called me giving two options: contact hospice or have her taken to the hospital. It was a Friday, and the nurse was leaving shortly, not to return until Monday. I decided to have Mom taken by ambulance to the hospital. The nurse had mentioned dehydration, and I knew that hospice wouldn't do an IV; denying her that could be a death sentence. My thought was that I couldn't have my mother die from dehydration or a bladder infection, things so treatable.

Later that evening, I received a call from the emergency room doctor. He had the POLST (Provider Orders for Life Sustaining Treatment, a more definitive living will) and wanted to confirm the "do not resuscitate" and "do not intubate" orders. We had made these decisions along with Mom a few years ago. It was a difficult task yet necessary at the time, and now I felt like I was being put in the position to make the decisions again. This didn't seem right or fair to be questioned while in a highly emotional state. I felt the "thumbs up–thumbs down" decision was in my hands, and I didn't like the feeling. I authorized antibiotics and IV fluids because she was dehydrated but stood firm on the DNR/DNI instructions. This poor woman does not have a desirable quality of life, but to let her succumb to a bladder infection seemed wrong. I'd much rather God take her home in a more spectacular fashion (his decision, not mine).

July, week 4 (238 weeks)

The day after Mom was admitted to the hospital, I logged in a five-hour visit. She slept through four and a half hours of it. Karen and I did lunch in the cafeteria and then watched a movie on the TV in Mom's room. Mom woke up and talked her normal nonsense, being pleasant, smiling a lot, and making her announcements of time (the clock was next to the TV). She didn't know us, was surprised to be in a hospital, but had no complaints (other than she didn't like the IV in her arm).

When we left that day, Mom was eating dinner. She hadn't recognized us and seemed worn out, but she was eating.

Between daily jaunts to the hospital, I took the time to contact hospice and pursue getting Mom signed up for the program. This hospital stay has been a major setback for Mom. She is so feeble now that she cannot walk and will require a wheelchair. She is only awake to eat and most of the time requires assistance to do that. She hasn't been out of bed for five days. The adult diapers she previously wore as a precaution are now a necessity. She is absolutely helpless.

We were informed Mom will be released later this afternoon. Mom amused us, wanting to be part of the conversation with the nurse and social worker, inserting words of agreement every so often. Even with her eyes closed, appearing to be napping, she uttered, "I agree."

Our plan is to follow the ambulance back to Willow Brook and meet with hospice representatives to sign the paperwork.

July, week 5 (239 weeks)

Hospice is amazing. It's no longer the program that I understood it to be. I had assumed you went on hospice when the end was very near. Now it's about comfort in your last days, weeks, or months. They have supplied her with a wheelchair and hospital bed. A lift is required to move Mom, and hospice has provided that also. They did say sometimes people graduate from hospice. I asked if there would be a party.

I don't know how much improvement Mom's got in her, but we'll take it day by day. By now, we're used to taking life day by day.

The reality is that Mom is very frail. She sleeps all the time, but even in sleep, she's thrashing her legs; it's not a restful, comfortable sleep. She looks awful; her color is poor, and there is a persistent frown on her face even while sleeping. It's difficult to imagine the end, but that could be the likelihood of the current situation.

I wonder if I did the right thing by having her hospitalized. I look at her and think that this may be my fault; I never imagined she would come out of the hospital having lost so much ground. I wonder if I prolonged her death rather than to prolong her life. I keep asking myself, had I known the result, would I have acted differently? Reality: there is no way I could have known. What I know for sure is that denying her treatment would have meant death. I know I would have carried that guilt for the rest of my life feeling that I killed my mother. Now I know that at her age and condition hospital stays take too much. By agreeing to hospice, we agree not to employ heroic measures; we choose comfort. We have decided that there will not be another hospitalization.

August, week 1 (240 weeks)

We've been visiting Mom daily. We don't know what the immediate future holds; she could survive this, or this could be her time to receive her ultimate healing in heaven. If she is dying, I have nothing more important that has to be accomplished other than to be by her side as much as possible. Karen and I sometimes go together, but often we take turns so that one of us is with her at different times during the day.

They are feeding Mom in her room because she is too weak to tolerate being moved. Sam has been very accommodating and will scramble eggs for her at our request. Mom doesn't seem to have energy to chew and won't eat very much, saying no after only a few bites. Initially, she couldn't even drink from a straw; Karen had to trap liquid in the straw and release it in her mouth. We get ice cream from Sam, and Mom never says no to that; I was afraid I was giving her brain freeze as I fed her spoon after spoon.

I have always said only babies can get away with staring; I now amend that to babies and old people. Early in the week, Mom would just stare at us, but it wasn't like she was trying to figure out who we were; it was pretty blank. Every once in a while, she would smile at one of us. The smile would just pop on her face without warning; it made us chuckle.

One visit, early in the morning, Mom kept licking her lips, and we interpreted that as she was thirsty. I gave her a straw in a cup of water, and she was sucking up the water with no problem. She drank like she had just crossed a desert. Then she tried to clear her throat and had some difficulty at which time, normal for her, she got very loud (she gets frustrated when she can't clear her throat or needs to burp). Currently, she shows her frustration by shrieking. The nurse came in (we refer to her as Lion Head because her hair looks like a lion's mane—and neither of us like her much, not even enough to learn her name). She yelled at me not to force water on Mom. Really? I'm tired, and it's a short trip to upset for me and an even shorter trip to tears. For Pete's sake, I wasn't water-boarding my mother!

After that incident, Mom fell sound asleep. We never got breakfast in her, and she slept through lunch. During the time we were there, the hospice chaplain and the masseuse visited. Lion Head stopped in again. I feel like everyone is "handling" us and wants us to "accept" that Mom is on her way out. They tilt their heads and speak in low tones dripping with sympathy. I wish they would treat Mom like she's recovering from a severe illness and not have one hand on the shovel. We are in touch with reality. I feel we're ready for the end, but it's God's timing.

August, week 2 (241 weeks)

We continued to visit Mom daily this week. Mom was making cackling noises one day (better than her banshee scream). She sounded very much like a witch. I was waiting for her to call me "my little pretty" and ask about my little dog too.

She is talking a little bit more, but we realized she mostly just repeats what we say. Mom asked who I was, and I answered, "I'm your daughter." She asked, "I'm your daughter?" And I answered, "You're my mother." She looked puzzled and asked, "You're my mother?" After repeating the volley again, I realized she was just repeating anything I said with a question mark at the end. It reminded me of that irritating game my sister would tease me with when we were kids, repeating what you said until you're yelling, "Stop it!" only to hear "Stop it" right back, followed by "I mean it!" and getting "I mean it" back. I almost expected Mom to start the "I'm not touching you" taunt.

She doesn't have much of an appetite and will only eat a couple of bites at mealtime. We've begun to bring applesauce and pudding with us, since she likes sweets. I told her I had a surprise as I gave her the first spoonful of chocolate pudding. I said, "You're going to like this." With a chocolate-covered tongue, she said, "You better believe it!" She finished off every bit of the pudding.

She still hasn't been out of bed, and I don't expect a full recovery, but she's slowly, very slowly improving.

August, week 3 (242 weeks)

They finally got Mom up in her wheelchair and out into the general population. She seems weak yet.

We went out to visit and help her with her lunch. She was in the activity area but sound asleep. She remained sound asleep during lunch. We ate most of her pizza (we tell them we're the official food tasters). We couldn't even get her to part her lips for ice cream. Today, she decided to communicate mostly with noises and grunts.

Right after lunch, they had entertainment; two people strolled about playing guitar and singing. Mom slept through the first two songs and then suddenly began screaming. We quickly removed her from the area, shrieking all the way to her room.

Mom's been screaming a lot lately, so I read up on it. Apparently, it's fairly common and can be because of pain or frustration and the inability to express either. It also can result from overstimulation. The recommended reaction is to take them away from commotion and provide a calming atmosphere (quiet, low light, gently rubbing hands).

Once back in Mom's room, I brushed her hair, and that seemed to help. She finally went to sleep again, so we left.

I laughed and said to Karen, "I guess we won't be complaining anymore that they don't offer entertainment here."

August, week 4 (243 weeks)

We're back to spacing out our trips to see Mom. She has rallied to the point where we are not worried that each day could be her last. I get there once or twice a week, and Karen visits nearly every other day. We try to go together at least once during the week so we can go out to lunch after.

This morning, Mom woke easily when we got there and said, "Oh, my daughter," when she saw me, but then she looked at Karen and said, "and my mother."

She didn't do her parrot routine today but, rather, came up with her own material, telling the aide she had nice teeth, and me that I had nice skin.

Mom has added commentary to her screaming. I know it irritates some residents when she lets out a scream. It is pretty frightening, having the quality of a tornado warning siren, starting low and building to a high pitch before winding down. I've heard residents tell her to shut up. Now she's doing that for them. At the end of her scream, she says, "Shut up." I wonder if she knows she's the one making that noise.

Lunch was one of her favorites, spaghetti. She was fairly drowsy and took a long time chewing. I found myself saying things I'm sure she said to me as a toddler: "Open wide," "Good job," and "Use your words." It feels like we've gone full circle.

When we headed out, the hospice nurse was there to check Mom over. She's also on the schedule for a massage today. Hospice is great!

September, week 1 (244 weeks)

Happy ninety-first birthday to my mother! We treated everyone at the facility to birthday cake; it was a big hit. Mom was alert on her special day and seemed to enjoy the attention she got from aides and residents issuing birthday wishes. One resident sang Happy Birthday to her twice (I think she forgot she had already sung it). At lunch, Mom announced it was her twenty-first birthday. Karen said something about her being old enough to drink, which got Mom hollering for a cocktail. I told her it was prohibition and it was against the law. She actually bought that. I don't know if Mom was trying to be funny when she claimed to be twenty-one or if she really believed it; either way, it was funny, and everyone laughed hard.

A few days later, Mom was difficult to wake and couldn't muster up a smile. We got her to wake up for lunch, but she wasn't very interested. She got very annoyed with us offering food. I quit after the first no, but she locked on to that word and repeated it several times with increasing ferocity. Yelling no soon became screaming, so we took her back to her room, a quiet place where she calmed down and fell asleep.

She had a good run; four days of eating, talking, smiling, and interacting. I didn't really expect she could keep it up, but at least she enjoyed her birthday.

September, week 2 (245 weeks)

Just when I think Mom is checking out, she renews her lease. We got there yesterday just before lunch and found her in the activity. She wasn't participating, but she was awake and watchful. After about five minutes into our visit, she said, "We're having fun." Mom was acting her old self, being very social, not only saying hello to everyone but also adding inquiry as to how they were doing.

Her glasses were missing as was one of her breasts. We found both. Her glasses were in her room, and her breast was tucked under her arm. I think back of the time she was so irritated because they had all her bras in the wash and she didn't have one to wear. Now they've given up trying to get a bra on her, and she seems fine with it.

I brought her to the lunch table, and she reached for the juice, drinking half the glass without assistance. They served peas, a favorite of Mom's. She ate several spoons until they brought out the watermelon. She pointed at it, so I moved from the peas to the fruit. After each spoonful, she said, "More." The entire week, she has said no to my offer of food, so to hear "more" was downright shocking and welcome. We finally ran out of the watermelon so returned to the peas. Even the aides were shaking their heads in disbelief.

September, week 3 (246 weeks)

On Monday, I found Mom up, not acting drowsy at all, but she either could not or would not use words. She grunted and cackled. She seemed to get irritated easily, at one point yelling at one person, "Get the hell out of here!" At least that's what it sounded like to me; she used no consonants. All her words, when she tried to speak, were slurred. I wonder if she was having one of those ministrokes.

I've thought she was on her way out before, and then a day or two later, she's greeting everyone and smiling and enjoying ice cream. I'm coming to no conclusions.

Before I left on Monday, I wheeled her over to the TV area and parked her next to Gloria, who was talking to herself. Gloria said, "Welcome!" and added, "It's nice to see you all here." I adjusted Mom's chair in case she wanted to nap, suggested she converse with Gloria, and said some words of farewell. As I walked away, I heard Gloria say, "Sit back and enjoy the rest of the cruise."

I returned to help Mom with lunch on Thursday. She was asleep in her wheelchair, and I thought it may be a challenge to get her to eat. She awoke and let me feed her, not having the energy or desire to feed herself. She wouldn't say yes or no; she just made noises for me to interpret whether they were positive or negative. Normally. she says hello to everyone who comes near. Today, she made sounds, rather witchy sounding noises that escalated. I asked her whose attention she was trying to get, and she nodded her head toward the aide across the table and said, "Her." All she wanted was for the aide to say hello to her. I told Mom that she probably had the words in her head, but, sometimes, they don't want to come out. She repeated that back to me. After lunch, I wheeled her over to the window, and she commented on the wind in the trees. She found her words.

September, week 4 (247 weeks)

The hospice nurse contacted me and suggested a change in Mom's high blood pressure medication, feeling that the high dose she was getting could be why she sleeps so much.

Mom's original qualification for hospice was acute renal failure. She is well healed from that episode, so they amended her classification to Alzheimer. I'm happy that she remains in the hospice program because they provide her with so much attention. Even her restless legs have even improved, maybe because of the massages.

A couple of days ago, Mom was out on the porch overlooking the pond with an aide. I like that they take her outside once in a while. We always get in front of her before talking or touching her (they lose peripheral vision and can startle easily). Karen got in her face and said, "Hi, Mom." Mom responded, "Hi, daughter." She has the occasional lucid day.

Today was a sleepy day. We couldn't wake Mom. We got her to the dining room table, but I couldn't get her to eat or drink. The most she ate was the three tiny spoons of yogurt that the Tylenol was crushed in. That was after a new aide expected Mom to swallow a huge pill with a sip of water. It didn't go well. Neither Karen nor I spoke up initially; I think we were a bit curious if this was even possible. Finally, I asked if it was in her chart to crush medications.

I have to remember that the aides are not nurses and this is not a nursing home. No matter how fatigued I get, I have to be aware and vocal.

October, week 1 (248 weeks)

A couple of times, Mom has complained about pain but has difficulty expressing where that pain is. We think it's in her mouth and mentioned it to the hospice nurse who will be checking it out. Mom lost a crown a couple of days ago, and I hope that's not causing problems.

Mom hasn't been screaming lately, but she has been noisy. Motion disturbs her, so anytime you're pushing her wheelchair, she's imitating an emergency vehicle siren. She's gotten repetitive, saying one word or short phrase over and over. What gets tiring is that she expects a response each time. She must have said hello fifty times yesterday. After a while, she added, "I love you," to the greeting. She loves us and the others at the lunch table and all the aides. Well, you can't get annoyed with that statement.

When I got there today, it was almost dinnertime, so I moved her to the table. Soon, a woman joined us, and Mom said hello, to which she responded, "How are you today?" Mom answered, "Fine." She had a conversation! Then a man walked near the table, and Mom asked, "What do you need, sir?" However, her tone was like he had no right to even exist, and the way she pronounced "sir" was as though it was a bad title, like jerk. I guess Mom had declared it the ladies' table. I told her that he only wanted dinner. She just grinned at me like she was proud of herself. She's getting back to normal.

October, week 2 (249 weeks)

A few months ago, there were five residents in hospice at Willow Brook. We overheard the nurse mention that fact and determined the style of wheelchair indicated which residents were in the program. Now it's down to Mom and Gloria. We're not certain what happened to the other three, but they haven't been seen in a while.

Mom was very vocal today but in a good way; she seemed happy. When we walked in, we could hear her saying hello to the aide. The aide would respond, and Mom would say it again and again. We distracted her to give the aide a break from having to say "Hello, Louise," every thirty seconds. Mom looked at me and said, "And you are?" to which I responded, "Maggie," and she added, "My daughter." That surprised me. She was very talkative, but, often, what she said made no sense at all. I would respond as best I could. She was also talking to her stuffed bear.

Later, Pastor Dan called to tell me what a great visit they had this afternoon with Mom. He said she talked and commented on scripture they read. She said the Lord's Prayer and didn't miss a word. They sang "Jesus Loves Me," and she sang along. When they sang "Amazing Grace," she made up a verse at the end that made sense. She had a rare day!

October, week 3 (250 weeks)

I began to wonder if it was it full moon on Thursday. We visited Mom, and the facility was nuts! I could hear Mom as soon as I entered the building. She was making noise, sort of a yelp. She wasn't in distress, just making noise. A resident made his escape as Karen was entering. She alerted the aide, and it took four of them to get this guy back in the building. Then he hung around by the door and kept pressing buttons on the keypad, searching for the right combination to open it again. This only caused the alarms to go off every couple of minutes. Then one woman who is supposed to be confined to a wheelchair got up and headed down the hall, leaving her wheelchair behind. They got her back in the chair and moved the escapee from the area, but then two more fellows decided to try and figure out the door. It was like everyone was acting out.

Mom was very alert and even asked where her purse was (she hasn't done that in a long while). Gloria was functioning pretty well too. She, however, suffers hallucinations and, while looking out the window, asked about all the monkeys. It was definitely a zoo!

October, week 4 (251 weeks)

While helping Mom with lunch, I spoke with her tablemate Warren. I've had some good conversations with him. He told me about the oil wells he owned with his mother until the former president's family stole them. He also told me that he was arrested and imprisoned for having diabetes, the county had taken his house but he expected to get it back, and he was related to a famous author. He watches a lot of news programs and today started the conversation asking if I had heard about the bombing. He added that it was good he didn't go back to his house because there probably was a bomb there. I told him he was very lucky that he now lived in a very safe place. He mixes a bit of reality, things he hears on the news, with his imagination and comes up with some pretty spectacular stuff. I have to admit I enjoy talking with him.

When Warren finished lunch, he got up to leave, and Mom wanted to know where he was going. When I answered that he was going back to his room, she said, "Oh, no," in the saddest voice with a frown on her face. I thought she was going to cry. I told her he'd come back and join her for dinner. She was happy with that.

I took her bib off and noticed something stuck to her blouse. I thought it was something from breakfast, but when I pulled it off, I realized it was two pills stuck together. I called an aide over and gave the pills to her. She in turn found the nurse. She crushed them and fed them to Mom in applesauce. This is the second time in a month I'm aware of them trying to make her swallow pills with water, and I thought crushing her pills for her is on her chart. I will be sending an e-mail this time to mention this issue.

October, week 5 (252 weeks)

I went to see Mom yesterday. She was sound asleep parked next to Gloria, who was also sound asleep. Mom's mouth was wide open, so I took the opportunity to look at her teeth. She's got a few molars left, and there was no irritation that I could see.

The nurse told me Mom's blood pressure was nearly normal now that they've adjusted her meds. She said Mom is not so tired and can converse again. I figured I'd test it out, so I told her about my weekend. Her response after each statement I made was "Oh, really?" It wasn't much of a *conversation*, but it was interaction, and I'll take that.

I brought Mom a treat, rice pudding that was sweet and loaded with vanilla. She was like a baby bird opening her mouth wide for more after each spoonful. Close to the last spoon, she decided she had an issue with the texture and would stick her tongue out with a grain of rice on the tip. I was expected to remove it, which I did several times. I think I probably won't bring rice pudding again; I'll stick to chocolate pudding.

November, week 1 (253 weeks)

I found Mom in bed sleeping yesterday just before lunch. She woke easily. It's amazing the difference since they reduced her high-blood pressure medication. She awoke with a smile and began spewing compliments. She kept telling me that I was pretty and that she loved me. She said, "I have a wonderful daughter." I assumed she meant me, so I told her she did a good job raising me, to which she responded, "Oh, I did?"

The aides came in to adjust her, which she finds frightening and gets vocal about; but when they were done, she said, "Thank you," and repeats it until both aides acknowledge.

They brought her lunch to her room, since they couldn't move her to the dining room (the sling needed to move her was being laundered). She didn't need my help with lunch today, so I just watched. She used her fork and didn't seem to have any problems chewing. The dessert was fresh-baked chocolate chip cookies. She was covered in melted chocolate by the time she was done; I had to wash her hands and face like she was a toddler.

She fell asleep, and I snuck out. She won't even remember I was there when she wakes up, but for the hour I was there, she was happy.

November, week 2 (254 weeks)

While waiting for lunch to be served, I did Mom's nails. I took off the glitter orange and put on the bright red she selected. Karen picked out some beads and a bracelet for her. They don't always spend the extra minute to put jewelry on her in the morning. I wish they would, because I still feel she appreciates being fashionable.

After the manicure, I found a puzzle that was suitable for a preschooler. It had large vehicle designs with a little knob on each of the six pieces for easy placement. She struggled with it. A year and a half ago, we were putting together five-hundred-piece jigsaw puzzles; it's amazing how she's regressed. I don't think I'll try any more puzzles; I'll stick with manicures.

November, week 3 (255 weeks)

While we sat with Mom in the common area, we noticed a funeral bulletin on the bookcase next to the fireplace. When we looked closer, we realized it was from Gloria's funeral. We noticed Gloria hadn't joined the group for lunch the last two weeks but hadn't realized it was because she was nearing the end of her life.

While we were making small talk with Mom, a slender woman in leotards set up a boom box playing music and then began dancing to entertain the residents. The woman danced to swing, Perry Como, Elvis, and a few more songs for half an hour. Mom laughed and clapped her hands. Whether she thought this woman was silly or talented, I couldn't tell, but she was thoroughly enjoying the display. When I went to get a chair so I could sit next to Mom, she saw me coming from about twenty feet away and started yelling, "That's my daughter!" She doesn't always recognize me; I was pleasantly surprised.

At lunch, she seemed anxious to dig in. She ate really well, making comments on how good it tasted. I fed her stew, and she fed herself pieces of watermelon. Lunch was topped off with ice cream, which she always finishes. She expressed how full she was as they cleared the table. Then she asked when lunch was coming. I told her she already ate lunch, and she responded, "I did?"

November, week 4 (256 weeks)

When we arrived at Mom's, she was not in the common area, so we headed to her room, assuming possibly she hadn't gotten up yet. Instead, we found a nice young woman playing a guitar and singing to Mom, who was slightly reclined in her wheelchair. Mom right away announced, "My daughters are here."

We encouraged the woman to keep singing. Mom giggled and clapped her hands. We requested some Christmas songs and joined in the chorus of "Jingle Bells," including a dance of sorts. Mom thought it was "wonderful."

Soon, it was lunchtime, so we brought Mom out to her table. She told another resident she had two wonderful daughters. I was so happy she said that because the last couple of weeks, she's recognized only me, and I felt bad for Karen. I realize that next week, it could be a different story, but for today, I'm happy.

December, week 1 (257 weeks)

Robert is gone. When Mom moved into Willow Brook nearly a year ago, she and Robert became an item. He liked to walk with her, and, sometimes, they would hold hands. Since he wasn't able to speak, the fact that Mom had trouble conversing was not an issue. Robert entered hospice a few weeks ago (we observed that he had the special wheelchair). We noticed last week they quit giving him solid food; he was getting yogurt and a protein drink.

Mom is the last holdout, the last of the resident in hospice. She doesn't have any medical issues; she's fairly healthy. She did start her screaming again. If she says hello to someone and they don't respond, she screams. I asked her why she was making so much noise, and her response was "I'm making noise?" I told her that she sounds like a siren, and she laughed.

Karen and I visited Mom the other day and found her really sleepy. I didn't see that spark of recognition in her eyes. She still smiled and said, "I love you," but she tells the aides that too (covers her bases). She didn't complain, appeared to be feeling well, just tired. She had spent time with the social worker, and it must have worn her out. Then she began shouting, "Come on, come on, come on," followed by, "Boomerang, boomerang." We have no idea why; maybe it came from a dream she had. Shortly after that, she fell sound asleep. We couldn't even get her to wake up to eat lunch, only coming around long enough to eat about a half-dozen mandarin orange sections.

December, week 2 (258 weeks)

Mom was very talkative this week. We haven't experienced this in months, maybe years. It resembled conversation. She didn't recognize us as her daughters; we were "nice people" that she could "count on." She talked about how nice it is to have people who will help you in an emergency, how important that is. She added that she would help us in an emergency. I'm not sure how competent she would be in an emergency, but she was intent. She made lots of observations, noticing a car that pulled into the lot and wondering why the driver didn't get out of the car immediately. She talked almost all through lunch. I gave her a Christmas cookie (a Swedish family favorite) and hoped it might spark a memory. It didn't, but she enjoyed the cookie. She ran out of steam by the end of lunch; talking is exhausting. We wheeled her over to the window, adjusted her chair, and she was asleep in seconds.

Karen and I went out to lunch after the visit. We talked about how improved Mom is. We also talked about how we acted with Mom when she was newly diagnosed and the couple of years prior to that. We agreed that we didn't understand she wasn't capable of some of the things that we expected out of her, and we were unreasonably impatient with her. We freely shared our feelings of guilt at lunch. One good thing about memory loss is that Mom doesn't recall how horrible we were.

We often discuss incidents prior to the diagnosis that now we understand as indicators of the problem with her mind. There was so many times that created confusion for us, like when Mom quit attending lunches with a group of ladies from her church. She had talked about enjoying the company of these friends every other week, and then, suddenly, she stopped participating. When asked why, she didn't have a reasonable excuse. Now we figure she may have forgotten where a restaurant was or how to get there. It was easier for her to mask her incapacities.

From difficulty remembering a route to the inability to complete a preschooler's puzzle, Mom has drastically declined in the past five years. As much as she has declined, we have grown the equal amount or more in understanding and tolerance.

December, week 3 (259 weeks)

The Christmas party at Mom's place was tonight, a two-hour gala beginning at five. We got there at four fifteen to be sure to get a parking spot and good table seating (each of the twenty tenants was allowed two guests). We were two of seven guests, which is rather sad. We got a really good seat.

The place was decorated very nicely with festive centerpieces on each table. At five o'clock on the nose, a fellow positioned himself near the huge Christmas tree and began playing an accordion and singing. They passed out an appetizer of shrimp with cocktail sauce (we found some crackers for Mom because of her shellfish allergy). Mom actually sang along with "Jingle Bells." Then Santa and Mrs. Claus showed up. When Mom saw them, she belted out the loudest "Hi" that I've ever heard come out of her. She's so childlike so much of the time. It made us laugh. She was attentive and even fed herself dinner. We ate with her and were really glad we had decided to attend this party.

It was a year ago that we moved Mom to Willow Brook for a trial stay. I read a post I wrote on social media from a year ago and realized how things have changed for her in one year. A year ago, she could walk on her own, put together a puzzle, play a game, and participate in sing-alongs. It's been a wonderful year at this home; she's been treated with dignity and love. The progression of the dementia has taken her ability to walk, feed, or toilet herself. She very rarely recognizes us as her daughters these days. But through it all, she remains pleasant. She still smiles broadly and never complains. She continues to be social, greeting everyone with a high-pitched "hello" and repeating it until she gets a response. She is totally unaware that her life hasn't always been as it is now, so we take her lead and just roll with it.

Though we are generally happy with this place, there is the occasional aide who doesn't seem to understand dementia. Karen shared with me an incident from a few days ago when she had used Mom's bathroom and through the door heard an aide ask Mom what her daughter's name was. Mom doesn't remember and hasn't said our names in months. We've learned the only questions we ask are things like, "Do you want juice?" or, "How are you feeling?" We don't ask questions testing her recall; it causes her anxiety; we can see it on her face and in her body language. The aide told Mom that her daughter was just in the room and asked again, "What's your daughter's name?" Mom answered, "Louise," and the aide said, "No, that's your name. What's your daughter's name?" Mom answered, "Mommy." That's when Karen reentered the room and answered the question, ending the inquisition. I told Karen we really need to speak up at those times and educate the aides if they're not getting adequate training in dementia. We can do it nicely; just say, "Please don't test her recall. It causes her stress." No matter how many times a question is asked, Mom won't be able to answer it. The information is no longer there to access. If the aide thinks she's conversing with Mom, she's got it wrong. There's a different way to converse with dementia patients; you just make statements and observations and hope for a response.

December, week 4 (260 weeks)

We made our Christmas week visit to Mom's. She wasn't having one of her better days. She was asleep, slumped in her chair while an activity was going on down the hall. We wheeled her down to the group. Even if she doesn't participate, she can watch; she still likes being around people. We have such trouble speaking up; we keep hoping they will notice our desire for her to be a part of things. They were finishing up their activity, so we wheeled her back. She seemed disturbed to be moving and made a lot of noise that would escalate from a groan to a scream. After screaming, she would notice one of us and smile, saying, "We sure have fun when we're together." She doesn't recall our names and isn't quite sure how we're connected to her, but somewhere in her shrinking brain, she knows we're always together and it's been fun.

She was reenacting the story of Goldilocks at lunch, complaining one thing was too hot and another too cold (the ice cream). After lunch, we set her up by the TV and told her we were heading out, to which she responded, "I'll wait here." Good choice.

December, week 5
(261 weeks, 5 years)

We visited Mom today. She was snoozing in her chair but woke easily. She was all grins when she saw that it was the two of us who woke her. She said her usual, "I love you," followed by, "We have fun together." Often she tells me I'm pretty, but, today, she said I was beautiful. I told her no one ever has called me beautiful, and her response really surprised me. She said, "That's because they're jealous." Do I dare qualify that as a lucid moment? It's been over five years since I've heard her give motherly advice or commentary. She even used her normal voice, not the high-pitched voice she's employed for the last few months. She sounded like my mother. After her comment to me, she smiled really big and laughed. Then one of the aides walked by and said hello to Mom. Mom replied "Hi," with a big smile and then told us it was nice to see Doris (her sister who passed away twenty years ago). We just agreed with her. She was happy. I like the days when Mom smiles a lot.

January, week 1 (262 weeks)

I have this feeling that I should be happy, but I'm not. We received news that, on the surface, sounds like something to celebrate, but I feel more disappointed than anything. Mom may be graduating from hospice. The program has been so wonderful. Not only have they provided a wheelchair, hospital bed, medications, and incontinence products, but also, more importantly, they have provided extra personal attention and care. We have enjoyed all these amenities since July. Apparently, Mom has improved too much. I just can't imagine what it will entail for her to be without these services. Not only does it mean we will have added expense to provide for her physical needs, but also her emotional needs will be compromised. Most care facilities are understaffed; aides are spread too thin, and basic care is barely met. As often as we visit, we can't be there 24/7. Mom's quality of life, by our standards, is pretty pathetic. Thankfully, she is not aware of that fact. She exists; she isn't capable of doing anything for herself. I was happy knowing that her existence was at very least comfortable.

I called the hospice nurse on her case, and she explained to me the parameters they must follow. To stay qualified, she must show some decline, things like difficulty eating or speaking. She can string more than six words together. She has begun feeding herself again. She's actually gained weight (guess I should have kept those Christmas cookies to myself).

I was so proud of myself for speaking up the other day and asking the activity director to include Mom in the group activities, even if she doesn't participate. When the hospice nurse visited this week, Mom was tossing bean bags and had the highest score of the group. That was a sign of the improvement, which disqualifies her for the hospice program.

I'm disappointed that Mom will lose all the extra attention, but that's the way it is. If things change, we can always contact them and get her reinstated.

I just have to appreciate that at least when we visit, Mom seems happy.

January, week 2 (263 weeks)

Today's visit with Mom was full of laughs. She was wide awake, admiring her painted nails when we got there. She was thrilled to see us and was talkative, wanting to know why my hands were so cold. She was already seated at the dining table, since lunch was coming within the half hour. She had her juice bottle and offered us a sip. Soon, she became impatient and began banging her bottle on the table (that's how she indicates she wants food). Karen gently held her hand down so she would stop banging. Mom looked at her and said, "I guess you don't want me to do that." Karen laughed at her observation and confirmed she was right, and Mom started to laugh. We all started laughing, even Warren.

I was sitting between Mom and Warren, and I often chat with him. He's very interesting. Today, he showed me the paperwork that will put the judge who arrested him for having diabetes in jail. He claimed he had been experimented on and pointed at a paragraph on one of the papers (it was his admissions folder for Willow Brook). He told me he was being held prisoner and showed me how they track him (an old hospital identification bracelet).

Then Gladys, a new resident, wandered over to introduce herself. Her sweatshirt said "Incredible Grandma," so I said, "I see you're an incredible grandma." She seemed very surprised and queried, "I'm a grandma?" Then she leaned into Warren and asked what I had said, to which he responded, "She said you're a terrible grandma." I quickly corrected him and pointed out what was printed on her shirt. I returned to interacting with Mom.

Karen had bought her a children's book with few words and lots of pictures. She turned each thick cardboard page, and we took turns reading. After about the sixth reading, Karen suggested we put the book in her room until the next visit.

Soon, lunch came, and Mom fed herself using the utensils. She really has improved (much credit going to hospice), and I understand now that she must graduate from the program. We'll continue to visit and be advocates for her.

January, week 3 (264 weeks)

We visited Mom twice this week. Monday she couldn't wake up, no matter what we did, and she slept through lunch. Friday she was awake and alert, sitting alone at a table.

Karen bought her a *Curious George* book that she read aloud twice on Friday. Then Karen brought out a deck of cards, and Mom sorted them, all the aces together, twos, and so on. It kept her occupied. I wish the aides had the time to give her attention like that.

When lunch came, she refused to eat. I tried to get her to tell me why; not hungry? upset stomach? didn't like it? She couldn't answer. She was adamant that she didn't want it. We gave up trying. I don't know if this is an isolated event or a trend. I'll be paying attention. If it's a trend, it could get her back on hospice.

January, week 4 (265 weeks)

Willow Brook was really hopping on Friday. There's a newer resident who always asks when her family is coming to get her. Today, she was pleading with everyone to take her home. She repeatedly tried the door, vigorously pushing the crash bar. An aide was trying to reason with her, while another resident kept shouting suggestions, "Tell her she lives here, tell her to eat lunch, tell her to go to her room . . ." Another woman, recently back from the hospital, wailed and hollered.

Warren joined us at the lunch table and announced, "They shot Pete last night." Pete is a new resident who got in a verbal altercation the other day with a group of ladies who didn't want him to sit at their table (maybe that's why they shot him). It turned out that Pete suffered a heart attack and died. Warren, who barely has one foot in reality, sees everything as a conspiracy.

Mom was busy sorting cards and paid no attention to the goings-on other than to occasionally laugh at the wailing woman and ask what she was doing. Karen would answer, "She's trying to communicate."

I have to give credit to the workers at Willow Brook. After an hour, we were ready to run screaming from that place; they have to stay and finish out their shift.

February, week 1 (266 weeks)

I went solo to see Mom today. She was in the group activity, actively sleeping. It was morning devotions, and the aide was reading from the Bible. When Mom awoke and saw me, she got very loud. It was a happy loud but disruptive. I managed to quiet her and stroked her hand while we listened.

When the devotions ended and we made our way into the dining area, Mom made some statements that I couldn't make sense of, but she expected a response. I tried to answer with "Yes," "Sure," and "OK," but I must have missed the mark a few times because she looked puzzled. Me too!

I moved Mom to the dining table, and we read one of her books while waiting for lunch. She read aloud a few pages but got fatigued with it, so I took over.

When the food arrived, she picked up the fork and fed herself. She would often drop food off the fork and then pick it up with her fingers and put it back on the fork. She was intent that the fork delivered the food to her mouth. I headed out while she was working on dessert; ice cream—with a fork.

February, week 2 (267 weeks)

Mom's place was decorated for Valentine's Day with red and pink centerpieces on each table. In the middle was a stick with a Styrofoam heart that sparkled because of a coating of clear glitter. Upon closer look, I noticed bite marks on each heart. I suspect Roger, the bad boy of the house, probably urged other residents to "taste this." Maybe someday, the staff will figure out that everything they do, including decorating, should follow the same parameters as what would be appropriate for a preschool.

Mom was loud today. She was just making noise. She would look directly at you and go, "Ba, ba, ba, ba, ba, ba." She was very intense. Then she would imitate a siren. After about ten minutes of this, she said, "I don't know what the hell is wrong with me." Somehow, it doesn't seem right to tell her that her brain is shrinking. We just answered, "Let's go see if lunch is ready."

Inability to speak is one of the things we are to watch for that would indicate a decline. At first, today, I thought maybe we were there. That was one of the parameters that got her off of hospice, the fact that she could string six words together and make sense. Today, she made noise and nonsense but then strung ten words together making a profound statement.

While we waited for lunch, Mom busied herself with counting how many people were at each table. Lunch was a hotdog and beans. She wasn't impressed with the hotdog, which is much too difficult to bite with no front teeth, but loved the beans. You couldn't even sidetrack her with ice cream. Sam brought her a second bowl of beans. She didn't care that the ice cream was melting; she had beans! I imagine after her lunch of beans, she may be capable of self-propelling her wheelchair. She'll be making even more noise!

February, week 3 (268 weeks)

A new fellow moved in this week. He decided to join us at our table for lunch today. Once seated, as the food was being served, he announced proudly and loudly that he had just had a really good bowel movement. Terrific! Let's eat.

Mom didn't make any strange noises today or bark odd words. Last week, she wanted to be fed; this week, she tackled that job on her own. It appears that none of Mom's behaviors indicate a trend; each one is an anomaly. Hospice told us to call if things changed. We see no decline, just good days and bad days.

February, week 4 (269 weeks)

So here we are, five years since Mom's diagnosis by the doctor. We have experienced a lot of up and downs. This most recent experience of having Mom on hospice felt cruel for a moment, setting us up for the final good-bye, only to yell, "Fooled you!" We had prepared ourselves to be orphans.

I was not happy to have Mom graduate from hospice. I didn't see it as good news, since it meant her miserable existence would continue; they weren't expecting her to die soon. I have to accept that there was something to be learned, some preparation that I needed, by going through the episode.

I grieved the loss of my mother years ago when she lost her mind. She looked like my mother and sounded like her, but my mother was gone. I believe part of that grieving created the resentment I felt. I don't know exactly when that feeling left me, but I no longer entertain that negativity.

We will continue to visit Mom at least weekly. We'll find moments of humor, joy, and tenderness. We won't find fear. At some point, I expect Mom will go on hospice again; I have no idea when that will be or how long she will be in the program and if she may graduate again or achieve her ultimate goal of going home to Jesus. I have felt most all of the feelings there are to losing someone you love. I have only the final one yet to experience with my mother, yet I feel ready and don't fear its coming.